Victorian Canvas Work

Victorian Canvas Work

Berlin Wool Work

Molly G. Proctor

B. T. Batsford Limited   London
Drake Publishers Inc.   New York

For Ron

First published 1972
ISBN 0 7134 2647 0
Library of Congress Catalog Card Number: 70 180139

Filmset by Keyspools Limited, Golborne, Lancashire
Printed and bound in Denmark by
F. E. Bording Limited, Copenhagen
for the publishers
B. T. Batsford Limited
4 Fitzhardinge Street, London W1, and
Drake Publishers Inc
381 Park Avenue South, New York, NY 10016

Contents

Acknowledgment 6

Introduction 6

1   Berlin wool work and the ladies who made it 7

2   Materials 13
    Berlin wool 13
    Other threads 18
    Beads 18
    Canvas 20
    Unusual methods 23
    Embroidery frames 24
    Needles 26

3   Patterns 27

4   Samplers 47

5   Furniture 61
    Regency 61
    Victorian 62
    Chairs 64
    Sofas and *chaise longue* 70
    Footstools 72
    Screens 75
    Cushions 83
    Carpets 86

6   Pictures 88

7   1851 Exhibition 115

8   Stitches and other uses of Berlin wool 121
    Wool work flowers 129
    Knitting, crochet and netting 131
    Costume and accessories 137

9   New work and restoration 138

Appendix A   Berlin patterns from *The Englishwoman's
    Domestic Magazine*, 1861–4 144

Appendix B   Berlin patterns from *The Young Englishwoman's
    Magazine*, 1871–4 147

Appendix C   Advertisement of Wilks Warehouse in the
    Art Journal, January 1851 149

Appendix D
    The Husband's Complaint 151
    The Wife's Answer 152

Acknowledgment

My grateful thanks are due to many people for their help and encouragement: Mrs Humphrey Brand, Miss Edna M. Cole, Mrs Nancy Kimmins, Miss E. G. Paterson, Mrs Violet Wood, Mr C. F. Colt, Mr J. Ennis, Messrs Sloman and Pettitt, Maidstone, Mr L. R. A. Grove, BA, Maidstone Museum and Art Gallery; Mr D. Kent, Mr F. G. Payne, MA, Welsh Folk Museum, St Fagan's Castle, Cardiff, Mr P. Moll, Maidstone Public Library, Rochester Museum, Victoria and Albert Museum, The Needlewoman Shop. My special thanks to Mr D. J. Doak for his advice about furniture. Finally to my husband, without whose help the book would never have been written and who now knows more about Berlin wool work than most men!

M.P.

Maidstone 1971

Introduction

With the interest shown in nineteenth-century antiques, Berlin wool work has taken its place among collectable items. The amount of work produced was quite phenomenal because it caught the imagination of the new class of genteel lady who had the time and the money to spend on making things for her home, family and friends.

It is a great pity, but nevertheless a fact, that women's work has never had the praise or wide-spread publicity that has been accorded to men. Although there have been many talented needlewomen throughout history, one would be hard pressed to name even three or four. Even in the feminine pursuit of Berlin wool work, it is not the names of the ladies employed making the patterns or embroidering the chair covers that are known, but the men who published the patterns and manufactured the canvas and wool.

I have attempted to trace the history of this work from contemporary books and magazines and by examining countless examples in museums, private houses and antique shops. Unfortunately much information was never recorded or has been lost, but I hope this book will help to explain some of the reasons behind the great popularity of Berlin wool work during the nineteenth century.

1 Berlin wool work and the ladies who made it

Berlin wool work is embroidery with Berlin wools on canvas by means of copying a coloured chart known as a Berlin pattern. It was first called by this name when the wools were imported into this country about 1810.

However, the name actually covers a much wider range of needle-work and can include work using any type of thread or beads copied from a Berlin pattern and numerous kinds of handicrafts using Berlin wool.

Berlin wool work and other types of canvas embroidery are often erroneously called tapestry work but tapestry is woven on a loom.

True Berlin wool work is almost completely confined to the nineteenth century. It began slowly, soon after the turn of the century and caught the imagination of the fashionable middle and upper class ladies. It became so popular that it usurped the place of all other forms of fancy needlework for many years. Mrs Henry Owen begins her book in 1847 with 'Embroidery, or as it is more often called Berlin wool work'. The popularity of the work was due, in part, to the time when it was introduced. Something new was needed to occupy the leisure hours of ladies with very little work to do and although it was criticized and disliked by the art world, this made no difference to its appeal to the mass of the population and it was worked by all, from the Queen downwards. About 1870 a new fashion for 'Art Needlework' began and this gradually became almost as popular as Berlin work had been, but plenty of Berlin work continued to be made, right up to the end of the century. It carried on in a small way until the discontinuation of Berlin wool in the 1930s, although by this time canvas work using crewel or tapestry wools and other types of patterns had really taken its place.

For all its popularity, very little was ever written about Berlin work, except for directions on how to work a particular pattern or to criticize it. It is an interesting fact that nearly all its critics were from the upper classes who possibly resented the 'new rich' and their pursuits.

The little that is known about the beginnings of the work comes from two books. *The Art of Needlework* 1840 by the Countess of Wilton who was one of the first writers to realise the importance of a reference work on the history of needlework. She stated that in 1804, a print seller in Berlin named Philipson published a hand-coloured design on chequered paper for needlework. There had been designs on similar paper before, but this was different because it was coloured. *The Hand Book of Needlework* 1843 by Miss Lambert gave the date

7

for Philipson's patterns as 1805, she also added that they were badly executed and devoid of taste. Both writers gave information about L. W. Wittich who became the leading publisher of patterns for more than thirty years. Frau Wittich, his wife, was an accomplished needle-woman and an artist of some standing and she saw the possibilities of extending the sale of printed patterns. Many of their patterns can be found and they are usually of good quality, clear and attractive. the designs of Wittich were imported into England in small quantities by Ackerman (of 'Repository of the Arts' fame) and others, and this began what was to become a rapidly increasing trade with new publishers constantly entering the field.

In 1831 a Mr Wilks of Regent Street (see advertisement in Appendix, p. 149) started to buy good designs and working materials direct from Berlin, and also a large selection of the best French designs and silks from Paris. It was an immediate success and his shop became a favourite meeting place for ladies who wished to pass a few pleasant hours choosing a design from the many patterns and actual worked examples. The patterns he sold were all stamped with his name and address.

By 1840 the number of copper plate designs published exceeded 1,400. Many women were employed to colour the patterns by hand as they were only printed in black and white at this time; later, most were printed in colour, although the large complicated pictures were still hand painted. As many as 1,200 women were employed by the leading manufacturers alone to colour the patterns.

The sale of designs and consequently the amount of work produced, was greatest in Germany in the 1840s, when the Countess of Wilton was writing her book and she states that many ladies in that country earned pin money working (that is painting) the designs for a warehouse. Several other countries produced designs including England and France and the fashion for working the Berlin patterns spread far and wide to such places as Russia, Sweden, Denmark, Holland, America, Australia and New Zealand.

Both the Countess of Wilton and Miss Lambert criticized some patterns as being badly made and devoid of artistic sense but they blamed this on the standard of public taste.

To understand the enormous popularity of Berlin work it is necessary to realise the far-reaching effects of the new Industrial Age and to know how the ladies of the new middle class occupied their lives. As more and more people acquired wealth, the hallmark of a 'lady' became one of idleness; it was a point of social pride that the lady of the house and her daughters should pass their hours with as little domestic work as possible.

Servants were easy to come by and four was not unusual in a moderate-sized house. Even with an income as low as £300 a year, one servant, a maid-of-all-work, would be kept. The lady of the house would spend her time in the appropriate manner according to her social class and this allowed plenty of time for leisure pursuits, for entertaining and to be entertained.

About 1850, each day would follow a distinct pattern. During the week, a mistress with several servants, would visit the kitchen after breakfast and discuss the menus for the day. She might employ a governess for her children or spend some time in the morning giving them instruction. The rest of the time, before lunch, could be spent reading, doing plain needlework, painting or practising music. Some ladies would not read a novel in the morning as they considered an instructional book or a biography more suitable.

After lunch was the time for paying or receiving calls which were considered a duty. Strict rules of etiquette governed visiting and it was not correct to make a formal visit before noon. A visit of condolence was made when the correct time had elapsed since the bereavement, usually not until a week had passed and the family had commenced church going again. A visit for no special purpose required just the right kind of neat attire; and it was important not to wear anything too costly, as that would appear vulgar. Invitations to dinner were delivered personally, and after the event it was customary to visit the hostess within a week. If one had to call on someone who was just an acquaintance, it was sufficient to leave one's card. Incidentally, ladies never put their address on their card. Calls were usually brief and if a lady was receiving a visitor she was not required to rise or see him to the door, and it was quite permissible to continue with fancy needlework, it was to be encouraged, in fact, if the caller was a gentleman, to show how accomplished the ladies were.

Tea was not a formal meal at the beginning of the century, in fact it was often not taken at all, but as dinner became later and later it was necessary to have something to sustain hunger, and it gradually became a favourite Victorian meal with a delicious array of scones, cakes, buns and muffins.

Dinner was the most important meal of the day, with three, four or even five courses and it went on long into the evening. However there was always time to return to the drawing room for conversation, music, or the reading aloud from a well-loved book, and during this time the ladies could spend it usefully, employed at their fancy needlework.

It was quite the custom for ladies to take their needlework with them to private gatherings and even to public assemblies and pretty little bags or small cases were made to contain the work. These cases were made of many different attractive materials including Tunbridge Ware (see Chapter 5, p. 72) or leather inlaid with ivory or velvet, and were just large enough to hold a few needlework tools and a Berlin pattern and piece of canvas, or a piece of crochet or tatting. Some suggestions for tiny patterns to be carried about in a travelling bag were included in the magazines. At a mixed card or gaming party, it was only the men and a few women who played and so special chairs and tables would be set aside for the ladies to converse with each other as they did their needlework. There is a mention of a party at Brighton attended by King William IV with Queen Adelaide and at this gathering the Queen, who was an accomplished needlewoman, sewed with the ladies.

Not only the ladies who lived in towns had these rather artificial lives. The wives of wealthy farmers no longer had the cares of the farm on their shoulders, no butter or cheese to make, no cows to milk, nor the full-time work they used to do at harvesting. All these tasks could now be done by hired hands and she could afford servants in the house, while she spent her time improving herself, her home and her daughters.

But for all these outward signs of respectability, ladies had to do some creative work as an outlet for their talents and they took up many interests such as water colour painting, playing an instrument, singing, and various types of fancy needlework.

One writer says 'A perfect lady should spend her time at sedentary occupations requiring no physical or mental effort.' No wonder, with advice like this and spending much of their time indoors, wearing tight bodices and boned corsets, ill-health was positively encouraged —as another writer puts it quite plainly 'the lady reclines on a sofa— languid, listless and inert'. How well Berlin wool work fits into a place in her life as all it needed was infinite time and patience to produce large and imposing masterpieces.

A distinction must be made between 'plain' and 'fancy' needlework. Plain needlework included making clothes for the children, one's own undergarments, and household linen. Mending was left to the servants if possible. Fancy needlework was crochetting, tatting and woolwork and it was 'a charming occupation for those ladies whose happy lot relieves them from the necessity of darning hose or mending nightcaps'.

Plain needlework was done by the poor man's wife out of necessity, but a social worker commented on the women who marry young, have a large family and go out to work in the factory—'they know very little about sewing and could not even make a petticoat for themselves'. Early Victorian underclothes were fairly plain, as it was taught that it was wasteful and sinful to enrich such garments—'the thoughts of a genteel lady should not dwell on such clothes'. Another writer agreed with this but put it in more prosaic words—'What the eye of a young man doesn't see, a young lady need not trouble about.' Later on, in contrast to the plain clothes worn by the poor, even the petticoats made by the middle class ladies were lavishly embroidered with bands of *broderie anglaise* up to eighteen inches deep—another pastime that needed more patience than skill.

In most middle class homes, plain needlework was done in the morning and afternoon only and not when one had visitors; fancy, coloured work was an evening pursuit but in a few homes coloured work was only allowed on a Sunday, when it must have come as a welcome change.

The England of Victoria was religious to an extent hardly believable to us today. The readings from the large family Bible, the prayers conducted with great force by the head of the family and the regular church going of the rich and poor alike were a new approach to religion after the deplorable state it had reached in the eighteenth century. The Evangelicals probably had the strictest code of morals and observance of the Sabbath, which included Sunday toys and Sunday needlework, but the High Churchmen also believed in strict obedience for Sunday. Their religion preached toil is next to Godliness and to be idle is wicked.

Needlework of religious subjects in this period had had its beginnings in the late eighteenth century, when popular 'satin sketches' were worked. These embroideries on silk, with the faces, arms and legs painted, were originally worked with silks, but during the first quarter of the nineteenth century Berlin wool was used and they gradually gave way to pictures worked on canvas from a Berlin pattern after 1830. Such pictures were considered very suitable Sunday work and were often hung in a nursery or schoolroom when completed.

During the Regency all ladies of any social standing were extravagant slaves to fashion, but as the century progressed the mark of gentility became one of sedate respectability. The lady spent much time and money making herself genteel and refined and how well these words describe everything about her way of life, her home, her clothes and even the novels she read. Victorian books on etiquette make amusing reading and show how times have changed with regard to attractive women. It was even unladylike to allow the sun to reach the face as rosy cheeks were not admired and only coarse country women working in the fields would allow their skin to become tanned, although on her pale complexion she would discreetly use powder and rouge and false ringlets (at 5s 6d a set) and artificial bosoms were on sale to 'improve oneself'. Another code of etiquette governed the use of gloves at all times and this must have kept hands soft for fine work, the poor servant with her rough hands would find the handling of fine threads impossible.

For many Victorian girls, marriage was later than had been the accepted normal during the previous century and it became usual for a girl to stay unmarried until she was twenty or twenty-one. It was a social sign of importance for a wealthy and successful father to have his daughters at home for several years after their education was finished. If a 'lady' had the misfortune to have to go to work outside the home it was a social disgrace and she was scorned or pitied. Music formed an important place in the lives of these young ladies and they were taught to sing and play whether they had any ability or not, for it was an obligation for them to entertain at parties.

Various occupations prevented the women from being idle, for complete idleness was not considered a virtue and they were no doubt diligent at their polite accomplishments. Talented amateur paintings and incredibly neat stitching show they took their activities seriously, at least most of them did, and it is rare to find a piece of shoddy work as anything not of one's best was repeated until a presentable standard was achieved.

Although the Victorian age was an era of great men, there was a terrible contrast between the conspicuous waste of the rich, both of their possessions and their time, and the terrible hardships of the poor. The poor had little or no choice in how to spend their limited leisure, while the wealthy must have been frequently bored through lack of an interesting occupation—no one more so than the middle-class ladies. It is no wonder they had to obtain satisfaction from their clothes, their homes and their belongings.

Slowly, a change came over these leisured women. About the time of the Crimean War nursing became accepted as a worthy position for a good class girl and gradually women accepted the idea that a good education and a worthwhile occupation made them independent and useful. The need for time-consuming pastimes was coming to an end.

It was not very noticeable during the sixties and seventies but by 1880, needlework, and especially Berlin work, was no longer an essential part of a lady's life, it had become a leisure time hobby.

2 Materials

Berlin wool

Most of the earliest examples of Berlin work which have survived were embroidered with silks on very fine canvas, as it was a suitable medium for the delicate patterns. In the Museum of Costume at Bath there is a waistcoat dated about 1820 which has been worked in silks with a distinctive Berlin pattern, repeated on both fronts. Several Museums have face screens of a similar date, with pretty designs of birds or flowers in silks, usually with the background unworked and fringed at the edges. At Bath, there is a particularly interesting pair made by Queen Victoria herself as a present for the Duchess of St Albans; one has a design of a parrot and the other a brightly coloured tropical bird on a cherry branch. All these little face screens are surprisingly light to hold. At this time some Berlin patterns were used for beaded trifles such as cigar cases, purses and garters.

It was not long, however, before a special wool for use with the patterns was being imported from Germany. It is possible that the arrival of Berlin wool in this country may have preceded the patterns by a few years.

Berlin wool came from Merino sheep in Saxony. It was taken to Gotha to be spun and then to Berlin to be dyed, as Berlin was an important centre of the dyeing industry in the early nineteenth century. This wool was particularly suitable for embroidery as it was soft and fleecy, without any twist and capable of taking brilliant dyes. But it was not strong, so only short lengths (no more than 305 mm (12 in.) could be used in the needle. It was also unsuitable to be wound into balls as this deprived it of its elasticity.

Once a piece of Berlin wool has been handled, even a short length on the wrong side of a piece of work, it is possible to identify this type of wool from all other woollen threads by the feel of it.

The fancy work shops, where it was sold, were known as Berlin Wool Repositories from quite early in the century until just before the First World War, when the mention of anything German was unpopular and even Berlin wool reverted to an old name *Zephyr Wool*, used in the *Dictionary of Needlework* by Caulfield and Saward 1882 where Berlin wool is called *German Wool* and *Zephyr Merino*. These Berlin Repositories stocked all the requirements for embroidery—silks, cottons, wools, canvas, linen, sewing tools and patterns, as well as small items such as ribbons, gloves and baby wear. They would also sell work which women had made at home and take a small percentage for their trouble, 2d in the shilling was quite usual.

Berlin wool was sold in two sizes, single and double thickness, in 1 oz skeins or by the pound; the larger quantities were proportionally cheaper. An advertisement in 1840 gave information about quantities available but not the price. The exact meaning of the numbers quoted is not clear but they might refer to the thickness of the yarn. 'Berlin wool dyed every shade of colour, the numbers run from $0\frac{1}{2}$ to 4, and can be bought in parcels of 3 lb, 6 lb and 12 lb and also by the skein of 1 oz.'

Magazines often gave the address of a Berlin Repository which would supply all that was needed for the Berlin pattern printed in that issue. The *Englishwoman's Domestic Magazine* in the 1860s gave the name of Mrs Wilcockson, 44 Goodge Street, Tottenham Court Road, as a supplier and quoted her prices. May 1861 had a pattern for a banner—a group of flowers on silk canvas at 9s 6d. January 1862 included a pattern of a bouquet of roses suitable for a seat and gave a list of what was required, 6 shades of pretty pink; 5 yellow/green; 3 dead green for faded leaves; 4 of fawn; 2 stone; 1 yellow and black; white for grounding. It adds a note that the violet flowers should be worked with 'ingrain Berlin wool which does not fade or fly as is generally the case with this colour'. Unfortunately this did not prove good advice, these colours were as bad, if not worse, than ordinary ones. The price for these 36 shades, sufficient for a music stool was 3s 5d, about 1d an ounce.

It was not long before Berlin wool was being made in England from raw German wool which was spun and dyed in Scotland and Yorkshire. Some was made from English grown wool which was harsher but harder wearing, but this was not liked by 'ladies of good taste' as the colours were garish, the only exceptions were the scarlet, black and some neutral tints. An American writer mentions English-made Berlin wool and recommends it only for groundings because of its greater strength, and for black as it was free from the smell of dye and cleaner to use than the German wool. Wool was imported from France in the latter half of the century.

An advertisement in *Needlework for Student Teachers* by Amy Smith 1894 showed the price of wool had risen. Tarn and Company who supplied needlework materials to schools gave a comprehensive list including Berlin wool: black and white $2\frac{1}{4}$d an oz—2s 9d a lb; colours $2\frac{3}{4}$d an oz—3s 4d a lb; shaded or Partridge 3d an oz—3s 6d a lb. Partridge or rainbow shades were very popular about this time and were made by Paton and Baldwins at Darlington County Durham up to 1938 when Berlin wools were discontinued by them. These wools were popular because they produced an artistic effect with very little skill, as the yarn changed colour every yard or so. They were often sold for children's french knitting which is made on a cotton reel with four nails in the end, and produces a circular cord. Some nineteenth century needlework boxes had an all-wooden tool for doing french knitting included in the accessories. They were made from one piece of wood with three or four tapering spikes in one end. It could be done on a cork instead of a cotton reel and is still called cork work in some parts of the country.

An advertisement in a magazine of 1911 *Everywoman's Encyclopaedia* recommended single Berlin wool for fascinators, cuffs, knee caps and mittens and double for slippers and golf hats. Prices were 3d an oz for black and white, 3s 6d a lb; plain colours 3½d an oz; 4s a lb; shaded 3½d to 4d or 4s 6d and 4s 10s a lb. In this edition of the magazine a Berlin pattern for an opera glass bag was given using Florentine stitch.

There must have been many manufacturers of Berlin wool in England and Scotland but very few names were recorded in advertisements. In a book produced about 1910 *The Little Girls Sewing Book* by Flora Klickman, she suggested using Berlin wool by J. & J. Baldwin for canvas work as 'English-made Berlin is the kind to get, as we all like to buy things made in England, don't we?' At this time Berlin wool was not really popular for embroidery and most of what Baldwins produced was exported to the Continent. They made four shades in 8 ply but the bulk of the yarn in 4 ply was in a considerable range of colours. It was recommended by them for 'embroidery and tapestry work and not for knitting recipes'. The firm of J. & J. Baldwins combined with John Paton, Son and Company in 1921.

Colours of Berlin wool

Before aniline dyes were invented all the colours used for dyeing textiles were made from natural sources: vegetable, mineral or animal. The art of the dyer is a very ancient craft and long before the nineteenth century it had reached a very high standard and there were an infinite number of colours possible. The chemists at the Gobelins factory listed 4,480 different tones for use in the manufacture of their famous tapestries.

Colours made from vegetables included the use of woods, seeds, flowers, fruits, mosses and seaweeds. For example, the bark of the alder tree gave a black, willow a flesh colour, a lichen found on stones produced shades of violet or green and another found on birch trees made brown, heather was able to give a reddish-purple.

Mineral substances from sand, ores, metals, rusts, and stones were used. From very ancient times red sulphate of mercury had been used to make vermilion and a certain clay for a greenish-brown. The dyers knew the value of shellfish to make red and purple and how to obtain crimson from a beetle.

All these dyes gave colours which would blend, one with another, without offending the eye, and most of the colours were very fast and long lasting. A stool top, embroidered with three guinea pigs, feeding on some cabbage leaves, outside their little wooden house, which was worked very early in the nineteenth century has practically identical colours on the right and wrong side of the work, except for the blue of the sky which has faded to a grey. Compared with some pieces of work from later in the century it is a marvellous example of the dyer's art. On a *prie dieu* chair panel, which is at St Fagan's Museum, Cardiff, and dates from about 1870, the bright pattern of scrolls and leaves on a dark red ground is only discernable from the wrong side, as the right is so faded that the design blends completely into the background.

Aniline dyes, sometimes called *gas colours* in the nineteenth century, were discovered and patented by Sir William Perkin in 1856. They were first manufactured in 1858 and it only took a few years to flood the market with the new colours and make the natural dyes unnecessary. Aniline comes from the Hindustani word for indigo—anil and was probably chosen because the first colour obtained was a purple, known also as *Perkin's Mauve*. In 1860 magenta was perfected in France and named after the battle. It was hailed as *the* colour for every article of dress and even recommended in the *Ladies Treasury* 1867 for writing ink. It was much used for embroidery, both wool and silk. The bright reds and greens available in Berlin wools made a striking background for the fashionable beadwork, in which the design was made with black, white, grey, clear glass and steel beads only. It is sometimes called *grisaille* beadwork as it resembles the painted designs which were done in Georgian times. Although the range of colours produced was very large and included some beautiful shades, most were rather gaudy if indiscriminately mixed and produced discordant effects. Most aniline dyes were subject to fading. It was caused by using the same mordants which had been suitable for the vegetable dyes and they produced unstable aniline colours. Until new ones were discovered they were always a cause of trouble because when the colours were exposed to sunlight they did not all fade an equal amount and this produced contradictory and unexpected tones.

Another cause of discolouration is dirt. and with the exposure to the smokey air of a sitting room for a hundred years this is understandable. It was not thought necessary to put Berlin pictures behind glass, and they really look better without it. Upholstery could not be

Presented with "The ILLUSTRATED HOUSEHOLD JOURNAL," No. 21, May 1st, 1880.

Dessin par AD. GOUBAUD, à Paris.

FLORAL WREATH IN BERLIN WOOL WORK

Adapted for a variety of purposes.

Hand-painted pattern by A. Goubaud, Paris, *The Illustrated Household Journal* May 1880   *Mrs Nancy Kimmins*

Plate 1

protected either, except from hair oils by the use of an antimacassar. The need for washing Berlin work occasionally was recognised in the nineteenth century and this recipe was given in 1880.

'If not soiled very much stretch the woolwork on a frame and wash with 1 quart water and 1 tablespoon ox gall. If very dirty use ¼ lb soft soap to ½ pt gin. A faded piece will be improved by sponging with 1 pint warm water, a piece of soap the size of a walnut and 1 tablespoon ox gall. It should be rinsed and dried.'

No complete list of the shades of Berlin wool manufactured by a firm have been traced, but a glance at any large Berlin picture will prove that the range of colours must have been very great, as it is possible to find several dozen in one design. For comparison, the list of DMC's cotton threads published late in the century contains over 600 shades. Twenty-six different greens are listed and each of these has a possibility of seven tones: ultra dark, very dark, dark, medium, light, very light, and ultra light.

Lady M. Alford, a founder member of the Royal School of Needlework, has some interesting comments about the use of colour in the home in her book *Needlework as Art* 1886. The Royal School was formed to commission designs from William Morris, Burne-Jones, Walter Crane and other leading architects and designers, in order to give employment to 'poor gentlewomen'. Her book was published when Berlin work was very unpopular with designers who were introducing *Art Needlework* and all she could say about it in her large book, was 'the total collapse of our decorative needlework came with the advent of Berlin wool patterns'. When considering colours Lady Alford recommends that sofas and chairs should be of a lighter or darker shade than the carpet and should contrast still further by the use of plain and rich designs. A touch of humour can be seen in her remark about footstools, they should be completely different from the carpet so that 'the poor thing may be spared the kick it invariably receives when the master of the house has tripped over its invisible presence'. In the eighties yellowy-greens and browns were very fashionable but Lady Alford suggested that careful placing of small items in bright colours would create a more attractive room. Aniline dyes were especially mentioned. 'They are offensive to the nerves of the eye and general colours should be pale. Reds should be scarlet or crimson tone, never with a yellow tinge; earthy colours should be avoided and with green there are few shades which are not beautiful except arsenical green which is impractical and repulsive. Yellow must be pale as primrose or gold as butter, buff must always be excluded as it gives the effect of yellow fog instead of sunrise or sunset.'

Other threads used on canvas

Silks for embroidery on canvas in the nineteenth century were sometimes used on their own but more often to add highlights to wool and beadwork. Raw silk was imported into this country in very large amounts and was not much more expensive than embroidery wool. It was made into many different types of thread.

On Berlin pictures, the use of silk can be seen frequently for representing water and human hair. In the illustration *The Finding of* 46 *Moses* about 1835, greenish silk has been used for the water in the foreground and white silk alternated with silver thread (now blackened with age) for that in the distance, both of these and the women's hair is in gobelin stitch. The silk highlights in the dresses are in tent stitch, except for the dress of the Pharaoh's daughter which is in a long stitch using chenille thread. *Chenille* comes from the French word for caterpillar. Two thicknesses were made: *chenille à broder*, fine, and *chenille ordinaire*, a coarse thread only suitable for a large mesh canvas. Chenille thread was expensive and only made in a small range of colours, but it was very fast.

Beads

It is impossible to write about Berlin wool work without including some reference to the use of beads, as they were so popular and many patterns were suitable for them. All the best Victorian beads came from France. None were made in this country until the second half of the century and these were often inferior and crude. The best beads were regular in shape and colour, although even in these the colours could vary from one batch to another and the worker was advised to buy all she needed for the work at one time.

Beads were sold at haberdashers and Berlin Wool Repositories in tiny glass bottles or small boxes. To make the work easy it was better to keep all the colours separate but, of course, they did not always stay that way and in the *Ladies Hand Book* of 1859 it suggested that a good idea was to keep each colour in a separate bag with the name written on the outside. A superb wooden box for beadwork dated 1810 is in the Museum of Costume, Bath. It has three trays containing twenty, twelve and fifteen, separate boxes respectively. Each box has a painting of an animal, bird or flower on the outside of the lid.

The smallest beads were sold by weight either sorted into various colours or mixed and were known as *pound beads*. They were available in three sizes, fine, medium and large, but only the fine and medium were suitable for canvas work, the large ones were for fringes and crochet.

The fashion for working the whole design in beads with the background of wool, either in full colour, or very often in tones of black, white and grey as already described, was much used from about 1850 on chairs and stools and for banners. In the fifties floral designs predominate with arum lilies and roses firm favourites, but by the mid sixties many geometric designs were being given in the magazines and were used on furniture especially pole screen banners and on the small trays with wooden edges and four small bun feet known in the needlework patterns as breakfast trays, The great weight of the beads did not matter on these objects and made banners and pelmets hang well. Naturalistic bead designs were still worked at this time and a very nice pole screen made in 1880 has black, grey and white beads worked into a skilful representation of oak leaves and acorns on a red wool background. Designs such as this could be bought completed with only the grounding to be worked.

Beadwork, in combination with Berlin wool, continued to be worked until the early part of this century, but most of it can be dated mid-Victorian. A lady who did this type of needlework as a young girl remembers that some of the beads were so small that even the finest needles, called straws, would not go through the hole, so each bead had to be attached by waxing the thread until it was really stiff and then passing it through the bead. It then had to be threaded into a needle to attach it to the canvas and then the whole process repeated for the next bead.

A quick method of attaching the beads was sometimes used but it was described in *Weldon's Practical Beadwork* as 'an idle way of working, it is an example of what to avoid, for, except for rare instances, no worker wishes to excel in this plan'. The method referred to, is that by which the beads are threaded onto a string and then couched down.

As well as pound beads there were pearls, bugles, metal and other fancy beads available. Pearls, either imitations or occasionally seed pearls, were used for highlights on Berlin work. The imitation pearls which were sold late in the century were crude and ostentatious. Seed pearls were used in working several of the large pictures of 47 *Mary Queen of Scots and the Death of Black Douglas.* One copy at Glynde Place, Sussex, about 122 cm × 91 cm (4 ft × 3 ft) is of the highest workmanship with a superb choice of rich colours especially a deep red. Pearls and beads are on the Abbot's mitre and pectoral cross, Mary's head-dress and crucifix and Sir Halbert Glendenning's sword.

Bugle beads are the long pipe-like ones, which are sold in mixed lengths. They are not often seen with Berlin wool work but are most attractive when used as a grounding, providing the excessive weight does not matter. Pelmets for the drawing room windows, covers for piano keys, bell pulls and the edges of thick table covers are occasionally seen with a design of tassels or leaves in wool and bugles for the background.

The illustration of the strip of tassels with a grounding of white beads came from the edge of a round table cover. 40

Although many Berlin patterns could be used for beads, the patterns made especially for beadwork have the beads indicated so skilfully by drawing, that they appear exactly like the finished article.

Canvas and other materials

There was a large range of materials available on which to work the Berlin patterns including canvas made from silk cotton, wool and jute, even-weave cottons and linens, cardboard and a fine wire mesh.

The earliest pieces were always worked on very fine materials, the most popular being *silk canvas,* which was made from threads of fine silk, wound round a cotton fibre. It was delicate and the mesh was even in size, which enabled the worker to omit any grounding stitches. This was not only left unworked because it was quicker to do, but because the silk canvas was itself attractive. In the *Lady's Handbook* by Florence Hartley, Philadelphia 1859, silk canvas is recommended for use when there would not be any hard wear, such as for screens and pictures. She stresses one important point about its use, the need to be very neat when finishing off, otherwise the ends would show through the meshes of the canvas. Two pieces of work which used to be in the home of the Marquess of Exeter are on silk canvas; a cheval firescreen with an elaborately carved frame has a brilliant parrot design and a picture about 406 mm × 457 mm (16 in. × 18 in.) of a girl with a St Bernard. At St Fagan's Museum, Cardiff, is another fine design with a boy and girl fishing.

Silk canvas could be bought in most colours but white, black, primrose, grey and light purple were generally chosen, the last two were recommended as easy on the eyes of the worker. It was the most usual canvas for work which was bought commenced, with the design in beads or wools complete. A very pretty cushion about 1848 in the Victoria and Albert Museum is worked in silks into a design with passion flowers, ranunculus and convolvulus and has gorgeous tassels at each corner.

Silk canvas could be bought in various widths from 13 mm ($\frac{1}{2}$ in.) for trimmings to 137 cm ($1\frac{1}{2}$ yds) wide for large pictures and screens. Four sizes of mesh were obtainable with 21, 29, 34 or 40 threads to the inch (25 mm). It was manufactured until the 1880s at least.

It is sometimes called Mosaic canvas in America and just Berlin canvas in this country.

The use of silk canvas made the design stand out from the background and especially when plush stitch, also called raised woolwork, was used to give a three-dimensional effect. The illustration of the parrot and flowering cactus is worked on silk canvas in this way.

pl. 3

Silk canvas can be detected by observing the sheen of the silk threads, which was occasionally enhanced by backing the piece of needlework with satin. If pieces of work like this are found today, the satin usually requires replacing and care must be taken with the choice of the new material. Some modern fabrics are too shiny, and do not look right behind the mellow colours of the old work.

38

Cushions, bell pulls and stool tops which have unworked backgrounds were worked on *jute canvas*. This was strong but still attractive enough to be seen on the completed article. Jute canvas is string coloured when new but it darkens with age. A pretty stool cover 501 mm × 356 mm (24 in. × 14 in.) on jute in a private collection has a design in tent stitch of full-blown roses in the centre and at each corner. It is very fine work. At Glynde Place, Sussex, a cushion also has roses on a similar canvas but worked in plush stitch with foliage in cross stitch and beads. This cushion is in daily use, and probably dates from 1870, and the fine condition of the unworked jute canvas background proves its hardwearing properties.

Cotton canvas was made in an even greater variety of sizes, one manufacturer advertised coarsest mesh No. 8 with 11 threads to the inch to No. 50 with 37 threads. However these numbers were not constant through the trade and firms devised their own methods of coding.

The threads of the coarse canvases were thicker than those used on the finer ones, but they were not all of a good quality. To obtain an accurate design it was important to have meshes that were square, regular and firm. France, Germany and England produced cotton canvas, of which the French kind was superior because of the accurate mesh and it was pleasant to handle while being worked; some cheap canvases were very rough. It is very difficult to distinguish between French and English canvas once it has been worked.

German cotton canvas can be recognised by every tenth thread being yellow, to assist with counting the pattern. It was cheap to buy and came in a large range of sizes and widths. It could be bought stiffened or limp and is frequently seen, especially on poor quality samplers. If it was used for a picture or upholstery with a very light or white background, the yellow thread was visible when the work was completed. It was sometimes given a sheen to imitate silk canvas.

The canvas which was the most popular of all in this country during the second half of the century was *double or Penelope canvas*. The threads are in pairs which made working cross stitch easy. Various size meshes could be bought but not in such a great range as the single canvas.

A very fine double canvas was used for an unusual pole screen at Glynde Place, Sussex. It is of a native warrior with an elaborate 68 head-dress and skirt of feathers. He carries a bow which looks as if it would have been more suitable in the hands of a medieval archer; the string is made from a length of black thread attached only at either end. The background is worked, but a few worn patches expose the canvas.

The size of the canvas mesh alters the size of the finished design and examples where too coarse a mesh have been chosen for speed, spoil the pattern. There are many chairs, stools and cushions with embroidered flowers, which are huge, much larger than life and they look grotesque instead of beautiful. In St Fagan's Museum, Cardiff, there are three interesting copies of the same design *The Shunamite's Son*. Two are about 81 cm × 61 cm (32 in. × 28 in.) on a fine canvas; one of these is not well stitched but the other has a high standard of workmanship and choice of colour. Very fine tent stitches have been used for the faces. The third example is approximately 152 cm × 122 cm (60 in. × 48 in.) on a very coarse mesh, which made the picture so large that an extra strip of canvas had to be added to get the whole picture in. Although similar shades of colour to the other pictures were used, they are in such large patches that the effect is crude.

Woollen canvas was manufactured in Germany and England and was sometimes sold under the name *Bolting*. It was never very popular but is sometimes seen on children's samplers.

Java canvas was more of an even-weave cloth than a true meshed canvas, with the threads forming an attractive basket work pattern. There was no need to work a background. It was very pliable and was sold in plain colours to be sewn with wool or silk threads in various stitches—herringbone, chain, feather-stitch and cross stitch, the latter was the most common. Geometric patterns were popular with the pale colour of the canvas showing behind them. It was made into mats, work bags, music bags and similar items that needed frequent washing including 'the ornamental towel suspended in front of the useful towel in the bedroom'. The illustration of the little dog 52 standing on a tuffett of grass is worked in wool and silk on Java canvas. It is a design frequently worked for Berlin pictures. A pattern for a similar dog was published by Hertz and Wenener of Berlin and is in the Victoria and Albert Museum.

Cardboard work is very simple. The cardboard was bought in sheets with regular holes punched in it and it was easily cut up and decorated with little Berlin patterns and words. Most examples in this country are texts or Bible markers with such pious words as:

(No cross—no crown), 'May we meet in Heaven' and 'For my dear mother 1842'. It appears to have been used more imaginatively in America where it was made into quite elaborate pictures. An American writer in 1880 thought the cardboard came from Germany.

Pieces of Berlin work were done on fine *wiremesh*, but it was not a good medium for withstanding wear. Any bending caused the paint to come off the wire, which eventually went rusty and broke. There is very little about now. Small face screens were embroidered in this way but they were not as light in weight as those on silk canvas. The sharp edges had to be bound with ribbon and the wrong side backed with silk material to hide the ends of wool. Napkin rings with a crude circle of flowers were finished with a metal strip to cover the edges, as these were sold made up into a ring they must have been very difficult to embroider.

Canvas available in America

A very comprehensive list was given in *Needlecraft Artistic and Practical* published in New York by Buttericks in 1889. Not all the materials were suitable for use with Berlin wool but all were capable of being used with the squared patterns. Plain worsted was used for what was called 'ordinary work' for furniture and was similar to Penelope double canvas and silk canvas was used for 'inspection rather than service'. Other types were Java canvas; Panama canvas— a stiff straw like material; honeycomb; railroad—with a large open mesh for quick work; mummy canvas with a close irregular mesh and Ida canvas with a loose one. Rugs were worked on a sacking cloth known as coffee bagging or burlaps, which was unbleached canvas on which cross or star stitch was suitable.

Unusual methods

Berlin work is sometimes seen worked on a piece of plain woollen material, usually of a dark brown or black colour. This was worked by fixing the piece of material in an embroidery frame, an essential item for this process, placing the canvas on top of it and tacking them together around the edges. The design was worked from a pattern

23

in the usual way with the needle going through both thicknesses of material. When the work was complete all the canvas threads were pulled out, one at a time, leaving the design on the woollen cloth. The illustration of the wreath of flowers from St Fagan's museum, Cardiff, 67 was worked in this way on black flannel. This method of working is most effective with brilliantly coloured designs. There is an illustration of a gay parrot on black broadcloth cushion from Pennsylvania, 1860 in *American Needlework* by G. B. Harbeson. A most attractive picture of *Dash*, the Queen's pet King Charles spaniel, is in the Victoria and Albert Museum; it is on cream flannel and the dog sitting on his tasselled cushion is beautifully worked.

Another method for achieving a similar effect was done by embroidering the design on a fairly coarse canvas which was then cut out and mounted on to upholstery velvet by applique. A chair of the mid-Victorian period re-upholstered in a dull greeny-yellow has an applied design worked in double cross stitch. It is interesting that the design of this pattern is identical to one used on Crown Derby china.

Embroidery frames

There are two types of embroidery frame, the tambour ring and the square or slate frame. The tambour frame in which the material is stretched between two wooden rings would only be suitable for very small pieces of canvas work, as if any part of the finished work was squashed between the rings it would be spoilt. They are either held in the hand or are fixed to a wooden stand. It is not known to what extent they were used for nineteenth century canvas work.

The square frame was used and recommended for doing Berlin work. If canvas work is held in the hand to be stitched, it will pull out of shape and the stitches will not be as even, as when a frame is used. From examining pieces of work that are not fixed to a stretcher (a wooden frame) it is easy to tell how they were done.

Square embroidery frames have not changed since the eighteenth century and apart from superficial decoration are identical to those made today. The simplest types were not on a stand, just upright bars with webbing nailed on and horizontal stretchers, with holes for little pegs, which were slotted through the uprights. They were satisfactory for small pieces of work. An interesting frame was illustrated in the *Handbook of Needlework* 1843 and described as for use with Berlin work. It is on a very elaborately carved stand with a wire or cane basket half way up each leg to hold the wools. The frame has webbing on the horizontal stretchers on which a large piece of work could be wound. The uprights were turned with a screw thread and secured with wooden nuts. It was only necessary to wind part of the canvas round the stretchers if the work was too large for the frame. The frame illustrated is very similar to this. It is at The Mount Vernon ladies Association of the Union, Virginia, USA, made about 1840 but the carving is not quite so elaborate as on the English frame.

A picture of *The Farmyard* 122 cm × 152 cm (48 in. × 60 in.) in the author's collection is known to have been worked on a frame. It was worked by a man who was a British Electrical Engineer in India and finished at about the turn of the century. The pattern, canvas and wools were ordered direct from Berlin. (It is interesting to note that another copy of this picture dated 1850 is in the Belfast Museum and Art Gallery and illustrated in Barbara Morris's *Victorian Embroidery*. It shows how long some of these patterns remained available.) The gentleman worker cut up the pattern, and pasted it onto card, which was then fixed to the edge of the frame. The canvas was unrolled to expose just the section to be worked and this was completed before the next portion was started. The picture was one of a pair, the other was of Mary Queen of Scots which was left in India at the request of a maharajah and is in one of his palaces.

1   Embroidery frame *c.* 1830, similar design to one recommended for Berlin work in a contemporary book. The Mount Vernon Ladies Association, Mount Vernon, Virginia, USA

Some embroidery frames were on very high stands and would either need a special stool or the worker would stand at them. A high frame is illustrated on a fashion plate of 1872 in the *Young Ladies Journal,* with barley sugar twist legs.

At the Great Exhibition, F. C. Grubb of Banbury, exhibited a work table and needlework frame in walnut 'of English design'.

Needles

The needles for woolwork on canvas were known as Tapestry needles but the work did not get the name *Tapestry work* until the end of the century when Tapestry wool was sold.

In the nineteenth century needles were made from steel wire which was cut into short lengths, each sufficient to make two needles, these were collected into bundles and straightened. The grinder then took a handful and rotated them on a grindstone to make points, afterwards they were cut in two, flattened at one end and had an eye punched by a machine. This last process was often done by children. The roughness was removed by filing and they were polished by travelling across a horizontal table with an abrasive and oil. When they had been scoured they were ready to be fixed into paper packets.

The blunt tapestry needles with oval eyes were sold in sizes 14 (the smallest) to 25.

In the *Dictionary of Needlework* it was recommended that gold or silver needles should be purchased for doing wool work in hot countries.

3 Patterns

A Berlin pattern is a printed and coloured design on squared paper. It is used by copying each coloured square with one stitch in the appropriate coloured thread or with a bead.

Berlin patterns were first produced for canvas embroidery at the beginning of the nineteenth century in 1804 or 5, but there were paper patterns long before this. The Italians and French produced prints for needlework as early as the sixteenth century but most of these were for cut work and 'spot motifs' which were transferred onto the material by pricking and pouncing. In this method the outline of the design on the paper is pricked at close intervals with a sharp point and pounce, a light or dark powder, is rubbed through the holes onto the material. When the paper is removed, the dots of powder are joined together with pen and ink or paint. However, patterns were made which were similar to Berlin patterns, although they were not coloured. In the British Museum there is a book printed in Paris in 1578 which includes about fifty designs made up of tiny squares; there are figures, birds, animals and scrolling patterns and some of them have the number of squares, which are to be used, counted,— for example a pelican is 70 stitches long and 65 stitches high; a peacock 65 stitches long and 61 stitches high. Another early book *The Needles Excellency* also contains patterns very similar to those produced by the German printers in the nineteenth century, but it is rare to find any indication about the choice of colour or threads.

The new idea with Berlin patterns was that they were always coloured, by hand at first, but printed when it was possible to do them cheaply.

The designs were first prepared by an artist. Some were original paintings but most were reproductions and adaptations from another's work. Up until 1842 any design could be copied without permission or payment, but the Registration of Designs Act was imposed to prevent this. Many Berlin pictures were taken from well known paintings and designs made up of tiny squares to imitate Berlin patterns appeared on textiles, wallpaper and ceramics. Examples of Berlin patterns on textiles were made very early in the nineteenth century, either exact copies or just imitations of the fashion that was sweeping the country. Barbara Morris in *Victorian Embroidery* writes of such a design on an English printed cotton in 1805, only one year after the introduction of the patterns in Berlin. The very popular Berlin picture of the Prince of Wales dressed in tartan with his foot resting on a large dog was used on a roller printed cotton in 1847 by Kershaw, Leese and Sidebottom of Manchester.

A floral pattern in squares, exactly imitating the popular designs for upholstery, was printed on wallpaper by C. H. and E. Potter of Darwen, Lancashire in 1852. On ceramics, J. K. Knight and G. Elkin of Foley Potteries had a popular series entitled *Baronial Halls* in 1840, of which several, if not all were available as Berlin patterns, and a Chinese scene published by Wittich had its counterpart on a blue and white plate. The list of designs which appeared in several mediums is endless and copying, with and without permission, was done on a very large scale.

The best patterns were prepared by gifted men and women who could afford to spend time producing designs of great delicacy, but when the trade was at its height, unskilled hands were all too often employed to satisfy the demands of the needlewomen. For hand painted patterns, the design was etched onto copper plates, which had previously been ruled with parallel lines in each direction to imitate the threads of the canvas. Paper printed with these lines was known as point paper. When the design had been printed onto a good quality paper, the colouring was done by girls, many thousands of whom were employed. To help the girls choose the exact shade required, a system of coding was evolved and this may sometimes be seen on the pattern. The actual colour was not given, only whether it was to be a dark, medium or light shade. These codes appear very complicated and were not common to all the trade, each printer inventing his own marks, but for example of the kinds of code used, a dot in a square might mean the palest shade; a diagonal from left to right—fairly light; a diagonal from right to left—medium; a cross—fairly dark and a V very dark. The colourists used a brush with a square cut end, and had several identical patterns in front of them, filling in one colour at a time on all the patterns. When chinese white was used, on its own, or mixed with other colours, and black, it produced an opaque patch which obliterated the lines on the paper making counting the number of stitches difficult. Some printers did not worry about this, but others had the lines re-drawn by hand after painting. Various paints were used for colouring patterns by hand, including a very unstable powder colour, but the use of water colour gave the clearest designs.

To simplify the choice of wools or other threads, several pattern makers instructed the girls to put a blob of each colour used, at the bottom of the sheet of paper and some included a separate strip of squares for this on the sheet. A banner pattern with a design of rose buds, given away with the *Englishwoman's Domestic Magazine* 1869 had five blobs of pink shades and five of green. A design in a French journal *Magasin des Demoiselles* 1851, with a wreath of mixed flowers,

2 Hand painted pattern 330 mm × 380 mm (13 in. × 15 in.) *Victoire Cousay 1835* written on the back

had so many different colours the strip of coloured squares reached from one side of the pattern to the other.

It is difficult to date hand painted patterns, but they were made prior to those coloured by printing and continued to be produced throughout the nineteenth century. The majority of them have the printers name and a serial number but the lower numbers do not necessarily precede the higher ones, as it is the practice of manufacturers to use the first one or two numbers for identification of a special set. The existence of such a large number as 17244 on a pattern of a dog by Hertz and Wenerer, Berlin, would be quite impossible, if the designs were numbered chronologically from one. Two patterns for chairs with religious symbols made by L. W. Wittich in the Victoria and Albert Museum are numbered 2930 and 2931, and this probably implied that they were numbers 30 and 31 in set 29. The date was printed so rarely onto these patterns, that when a pattern is seen with a number in the 1800s such as 1860 on a design of a humming bird with magnolias, this is more likely to be its serial number than the date. However, the date when the pattern was worked was sometimes written in ink or pencil on the back. Generally, the earliest patterns have the softest colours, but colours varied considerably from one batch to another from the same printer, and some always chose harsh colours for their work.

Patterns were available from many Berlin Wool Repositories throughout the country and they could be ordered direct from suppliers in Germany. The name of T. Wilks, 186 Regent Street, is written in ink or stamped onto many patterns that have survived and there is no doubt that he was the most well-known importer and retailer.

Names of other suppliers are known because of their advertisements in newspapers and journals. In the *Art Journal* 1849 was inserted 'Decorative Needlework Establishment (late Miss Lambert's) 3 New Burlington Street, call the attention of Nobility and Gentry to their new and elegant assortment of designs in decorative needlework. Mesdames Purcell and Dolan respectfully solicit an early inspection of their collection as they feel assured that for excellence of material, novelty in design and arrangement of colours, their patterns are unrivalled'.

The patterns which were given away with the monthly journals are very numerous and fortunately they are nearly all dated, which shows the trend of designs. As with free gifts today, they were not of a consistently good standard, in fact some were quite atrocious! The earliest patterns appeared about the middle of the century and many floral bouquets and wreaths can be seen in journals such as *The*

3 Hand painted pattern 330 mm × 380 mm (13 in. × 15 in.) *Argyll Repository Regent St* written in ink on the front, *Victoire Cousay Thursday May 5th 1836* written on the back *Mr D. Kent*

Englishwoman's Domestic Magazine, The Young Ladies Journal, The Ladies Treasury, and *The Young Englishwoman.* By the mid-sixties many of the designs in the most fashionable magazines were for borders with geometric or floral patterns or ornamental scrolls, but floral bouquets were featured occasionally. Some journals gave away special patterns with the Christmas number or a pair of patterns with the December and January editions. They consisted of a back and seat for a chair, a matching pair of patterns or a picture to be worked. Many of the free patterns for pictures were very badly drawn by poor artists and were among the worst examples of Berlin work. *The Young Ladies Journal* always gave away special patterns; the two parrot designs illustrated, were given away December 1871 and January 1872, a few years later it was a child carrying holly and a lady selling flowers and in 1882 a pattern entitled *The Knight and his Lady.* All these designs were printed in colour.

11–14

Some of the designs which were given away were hand painted, especially the small ones. The size varied from about 127 mm × 76 mm (5 in. × 3 in.) which would go into the journal without folding to really large special offers up to 457 mm × 356 mm (18 in. × 14 in.). A great many of these patterns were especially produced in France for inclusion in magazines, and although it is difficult to generalize, most of the French designs are finer and more clearly printed than either the English or German ones.

Towards the end of the century Berlin patterns had all but ceased to be produced by the popular magazines, although they still appeared from time to time and it was still possible to buy them from needle-work shops. In the *Girls Own Annual* 1882 there was a pattern for the back of a chair and written instructions for adapting it for the seat. The design was of scrolling leaves and extremely difficult to interpret, as it was very small, about 152 mm × 76 mm (6 in. × 3 in.), and the colours for the Berlin wools were only indicated by black, white and hatched squares, printed onto cheap paper. Three years later this same annual gave no actual patterns for Berlin work, but there were several engravings of little gifts that could be made with canvas embroidery.

The names of a few Berlin pattern makers are often seen on examples which remain today, especially L. W. Wittich, Carl F. W. Wicht, Hertz and Wegener, A. Todt and G. E. Falbe. Unfortunately the records of these German printers have been lost and very little is known about them.

Berlin wool embroidery could be carried out from a drawing on the canvas, either printed or drawn by hand, without the use of a paper pattern. Although this process eventually took the market from the

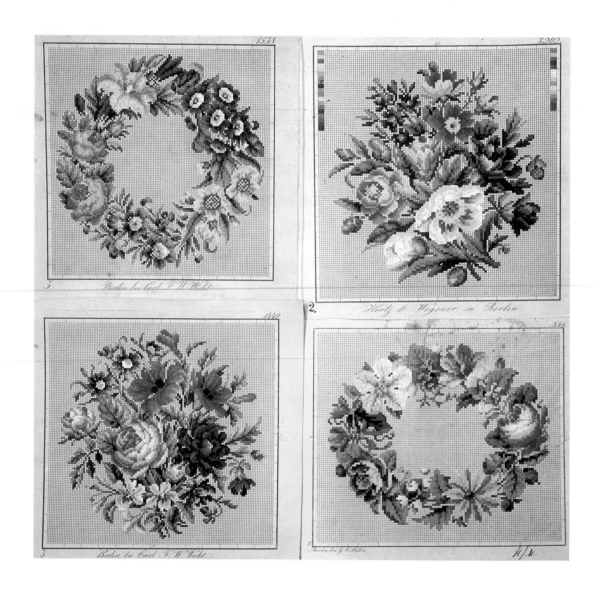

Hand-painted patterns by Carl F. W. Wicht, Hertz and Wegener and
G. E. Falbe, Berlin   *Mrs Nancy Kimmins*

Plate 2

4 Hand painted pattern 305 mm × 305 mm (12 in. × 12 in.) made by
L. W. Wittich, Berlin *Mr D. Kent*

prints, it is rare to find an example of nineteenth century work done
this way, because if the needlework is in good condition, no indication
of the drawing will be seen. A design on the canvas is most likely to
be found, where silks have been used with Berlin wool, because they
tend to disintegrate, revealing traces of the design. A piece of
needlework for a pole screen, about 1840, had been embroidered in
this way, as parts of the child and her parrot had worn where silk had
been used, and the outline of the design, filled in with paints could
be seen.

5　Hand painted pattern 305 mm × 305 mm (12 in. × 12 in.) made by
L. W. Wittich, Berlin　*Mr D. Kent*

The most difficult way of following a Berlin pattern was from
written instructions, similar to fairisle knitting. Many of these
patterns have inaccuracies, which made perfect work impossible
without much unravelling. This may have been the fault of the printer
or the writer, but they were so complicated, it was quite probable
both were at fault. An amazingly vague book called *Art Needlework*
by Mrs Townend had a chapter 'Tapestry and Canvas Embroidery'.
It had several patterns described and the author begins: 'There is
a very good shop where you can get almost, if not quite, anything
you require. It is in London, but I am not sure of the name, though
I think it is Kenning'. (Probably George Kenning and Son, Little
Britain, London, EC, who advertised embroidery materials.) The

6 Hand painted pattern 152 mm × 152 mm (6 in. × 6 in.) made by Hertz and Wegener, Berlin *Mr D. Kent*

instructions for a border and corner of leaves is given in great detail and takes eight and a half columns. 'First row. Two cross stitches, miss two, eleven stitches (the whole is carried out in cross stitch), miss two, make eleven, miss two, then eleven, miss two, make eleven, and for the corner taken four diagonally, then eleven on the straight again, miss two, then eleven and so on to the next corner. Second row. Make two stitches immediately above the two missed in the first row, two over the next space, two over the next space, two over the next space and now we come to the corner; do nothing in the corner, but go onto the next space and so on to the next corner . . . and so on.' There is no publishing date in this book, but it is fairly late and it is quite surprising to find the author actually praising large Berlin pictures and encouraging her readers to do them.

35

7   Hand painted pattern 330 mm × 380 mm (13 in. × 15 in.)   *Mr D. Kent*

8   Hand painted pattern for chair seat and back; made by Louis Glüer, ▶
Berlin (page 68)

9 Pattern for cheval screen printed in colour; 380 mm × 305 mm (15 in. × 12 in.)

From partly worked examples it is possible to see the various methods used by the ladies when following a printed chart. A commenced picture of a peacock is an example of an impetuous worker who rushed into the most interesting part of the design with no thought whatsoever. There is not even a centre line marked, she just began working the tail and this is nearly complete, but either she became bored, or found it too difficult to carry on. Some workers lightly sketched the design or put in the centre lines with a pencil or ink. This was a good idea when a central pattern was to be worked with a border or corners. Patterns for borders usually give at least one and a half repeats of the design, the Victoria and Albert Museum have several of these intended for shelf edgings, bell pulls and similar items. When working these long strips, it was the usual practice to work several inches with one colour and then several inches with another colour, gradually filling in the pattern and finishing with the background. For a design that was to be symmetrical or to meet around the edge of a stool or cushion it was essential to start in the centre and work towards the edges, but many examples of finished work show that this was not always done as the designs do not fit into the corners properly.

10   Pattern for slippers printed in colour. *Young Ladies Journal* November 1871   *Mr D. Kent*

11 to 14   Pair of patterns printed in colour and the pictures worked from them. Patterns 380 mm × 380 mm (15 in. × 15 in.) *Young Ladies Journal* December 1871 and January 1872 *Miss Edna M. Cole* (pages 32 and 90)

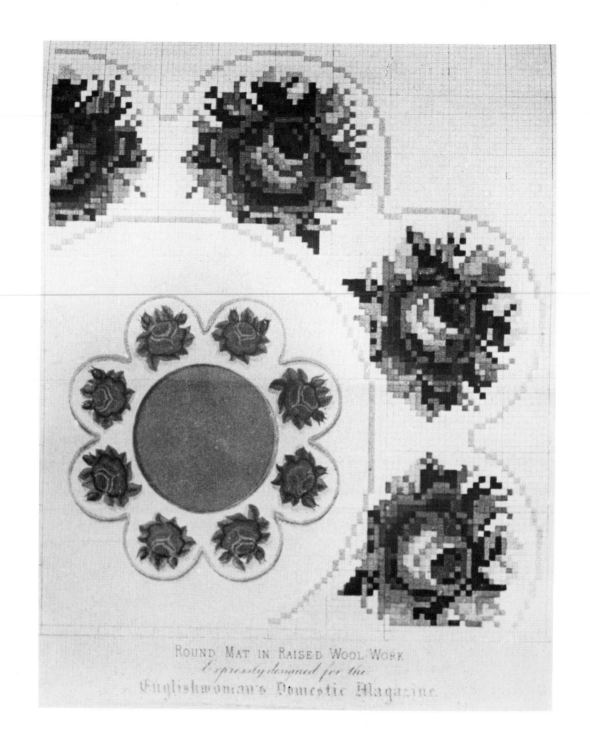

ROUND MAT IN RAISED WOOL WORK
Expressly designed for the
Englishwoman's Domestic Magazine

15   Pattern printed in colour for raised wool work 165 mm × 190 mm (6½ in. × 7½ in.) *Englishwoman's Domestic Magazine* January 1863

16 Pattern printed in colour for beads with Berlin wool grounding;
203 mm × 203 mm (8 in. × 8 in.) *Englishwoman's Domestic Magazine* 1862

17 Border pattern hand painted in brown and turquoise; made by Hertz
and Wegener, Berlin *Mr D. Kent*

18   Border patterns; small scroll handmade in yellow and gold   *Mr D. Kent*

19   Pattern printed in colour   *Mr D. Kent*

4 Samplers

Before printed books were cheap and easy to come by, the sampler was an essential part of a young lady's education. When she got married she would want to embroider her clothes and those of her family and be able to decorate her home with her own needlework, and in so doing, amuse herself profitably during her leisure hours. It was an accomplishment for the ladies with plenty of time for fine and beautiful work, not for the servants, whose roughened hands were only fit for plain sewing.

By the end of the eighteenth century the child's sampler had become an exercise in patience more than an introduction to the different types of embroidery. The designs of samplers used at this time and for the first seventy years of the nineteenth century are well known, with the border of little rosebuds or carnations, the spot motifs and the pious verse. The date and age of the child were usually added and this became universally accepted as a sampler which was then framed and put up on the wall by proud parents. Cross stitch was known as sampler stitch and it is rare to find anything else; most were worked on a fine linen or woollen cloth.

It is not necessary for the purpose of following the history of Berlin wool work to dwell on the majority of children's samplers of the nineteenth century but there are some worked with Berlin wool and others where Berlin patterns have been used. There are also some very interesting real samplers showing examples of stiches.

One of the earliest dated child's sampler in Berlin wool is in St Fagan's Museum, Cardiff. It was made in 1833 and has the alphabet and various little motifs surrounded by a border.

At this early date very few girls had a proper education apart from the upper classes, although the church and some charities endowed a few elementary schools so that some poor children would have similar opportunities to the sons and daughters of the wealthy. The state did not follow this example until 1860. These elementary schools taught reading, writing and casting accounts, one such school included 'good manners and other useful things'. The children did not stay at school for long, because of the poverty of their large families and most would be working before they were eleven. It was necessary for some of the charities to provide clothes for the children to wear at school.

Some children would be taught by the curate in the north aisle of the church and it is unlikely these girls learnt any needlework, as the poor man could ill-afford even a small sum for materials out of his meagre stipend.

If parents had a little money to spare, they could send their children to a private or dame school for twopence or threepence a week; almost every town and village had such a school. Sometimes the 'dame' would be a man and often the educational standard was very low with the older pupils teaching the younger ones. Many were just places to leave children so that the mother could go out to work and not real schools for the education of the pupils. However, there is evidence that a considerable amount of needlework was taught at some of them. In 1844 a school in Glamorgan, Wales, was visited by the Commissioners and they reported that the girls here sewed all the morning every day.

Sewing appears to have been extensively taught in Wales at this time, if the names of the schools can be taken as an indication—'Mrs Suetts, Reading and Sewing School, Llanstephan, Carmarthenshire', 'Wood's Row Sewing and Reading School, Carmarthen' and 'Lacques Welsh School for Reading Welsh and English Bibles and to Sew, Knit and Spin'.

The daughters of the 'respectable' families were educated by a governess at home, and from the earliest part of the century more and more women were employed in this capacity. In the census of 1851 there were 2100 women employed this way in England. Governesses had always educated daughters of the upper middle class and professional men, to prepare them for a successful marriage, but as time went on, the daughters of farmers and even tradesmen had a governess 'as a mode of advancing them a step in life' although this was regarded by the upper class as apeing their betters.

The women employed as governesses were extraordinarily underpaid and treated worse than a lady's maid. A London circulating library refused subscriptions from such women because of their poor salary. It is not surprising that these women and girls were often ill-equipped to teach their charges the three R's and relied on music, drawing and needlework to impress the master of the house that her salary was properly earned.

The governess would always teach her pupil to make a sampler and when it was complete it would be a pleasant change to take up Berlin work and make a cigar case for Papa, a picture to hang on the nursery wall or some little trifles for the bazaar. The development of the bazaar for various charities began in the 1830s and was one reason for the great increase in the number of little pieces of fancy work that were described in the magazines and penny booklets. Little gifts, both useful and useless were made for the 'cause' and they make amusing reading today. One suggestion was a tissue paper fly rest, another a paper shade for a standard oil lamp (one can only hope this

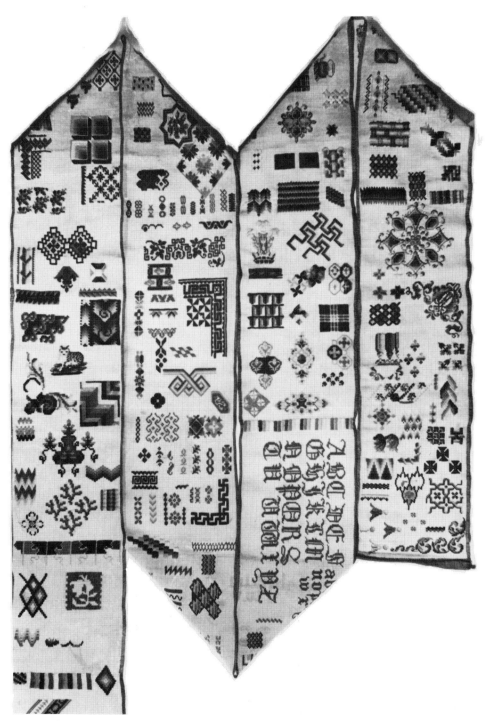

20   Berlin wool sampler 203 mm wide, 488 cm long (8 in. wide, 16 ft long)
on single canvas bound with blue ribbon *c.* 1850

was removed before lighting up!) Endless varieties of containers in every conceivable material were made. No other generation can ever have had so many bags and boxes. Small pieces of Berlin work were very suitable for a bazaar and a painting *The Empty Purse* by James Collenson 1857 shows two pieces among the array collected for St Brides Church—a pair of men's braces and a worked pair of slippers. It was considered very genteel to help Charities and mothers would like to give items made by their daughters. In the *Art Journal* 1847, there is an advertisement for a 'Fancy Sale in aid of decayed merchants, bankers, clergymen, solicitors, medical men, master manufacturers and tradesmen'. It takes up half a page and lists about 100 patrons, all of which have titles. They are appealing for paintings, music, books, shells, flowers and fancy work articles to sell.

But this sort of fancy work was only for the wealthy and until the State opened schools as the result of an inquiry into the education of the poor, only one child in eight went to any kind of school for as long as three years with any regularity. As a result of the building of State schools in every town and village, all children were able to attend school and towards the end of the century the instruction of needlework in progressive schools gradually changed from a routine exercise into something educational. Much of the delightful work is still with us, as the best exercises were kept as an example for other children to copy. Samplers of alphabets and numerals in cross stitch were still done as these were necessary for marking linen, but the most charming pieces are miniature articles of clothes or parts of garments which taught the girls the different processes involved. Examples of patching, darning and knitting were done also. Some of the pieces of work were sewn into books and dated so that it is possible to see the child's progress from year to year through the standards (not classes in nineteenth century.)

It would be wrong to imagine that this type of needlework was taught everywhere. Countless schools continued making the well-known sampler throughout the whole of the nineteenth century and even at the beginning of the twentieth century, the examples in Berlin wool can be found from all of this time, although they were never as popular as those worked in silk or cotton threads.

A sampler dated 1848 at St Fagan's Museum, Cardiff, has a verse, little motifs and a border, all in Berlin wool except for a little black silk. The colours are particularly attractive and unusual on children's work. It would appear that the choice of colours used on samplers was that of the children and no guidance was given by the teacher, as it is only very occasionally that one is seen where the shades have been carefully chosen to blend one with another.

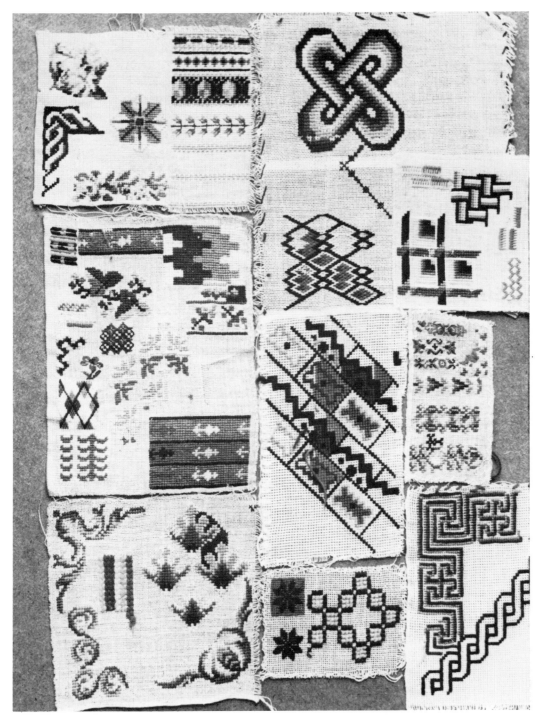

21 Samplers of Berlin work, probably made by a professional embroideress; worked on many types of canvas with a variety of threads

Berlin wool samplers made in the fifties and sixties were very little changed from the earlier ones, but they sometimes include some little chequered patterns, probably copied from a magazine. These are usually well placed on the canvas showing the artistic taste of the teacher or the child, and a desire to do something new, rather than copying from old samplers and pattern books which was the usual procedure. One of these is illustrated, it has no date but is probably 22 mid-century as this is the time that such patterns appeared in the magazines, the two candles and the monstrance might be the influence of a convent school. It is a Belgian sampler but in no way different from English ones of a similar date.

Some samplers have designs copied from fine silk examples but the use of Berlin wool makes a very clumsy piece of work. At St Fagan's is an undated piece with an alphabet, Adam and Eve and an altar with IHS in the centre (another convent possibly) and the author has a similar one with Adam and Eve, the Tree of Life and a coarse carnation (?) border.

Berlin wool samplers from the first half of the century are usually worked on a fine single canvas, the later ones on a double canvas 10 squares to the inch. The size of the sampler was determined by the width of the canvas and very similar to those worked in silk or cotton on woollen or linen cloth, but some very large ones were made in Wales using a large mesh canvas. The large samplers were popular at the end of the century, when some large pictures were worked on similar canvas; 762 mm $\times$ 914 mm (30 in. $\times$ 36 in.) was not uncommon and an example 1219 mm $\times$ 1219 mm (48 in. $\times$ 48 in.) has letters 25 mm (1 inch) high giving a verse in English and Welsh surrounded with a border of roses. Most Welsh samplers seem to have kept the original colours of the Berlin wool better than the majority of English ones, possibly due to the small windows in the cottages.

The samplers made in the twentieth century with Berlin wool, were obviously worked at a school with an elderly teacher, as they were not included in the published needlework schemes for State schools, even in the 1890s. A sampler dated 1912 worked on double canvas has a central design of a boy in a rural setting, surrounded by a border of roses; the one illustrated by Elizabeth Jones is very 23 similar to this, the leaf border and the two enormous birds are taken from an early pattern, but the two lovers could have been designed at any time. Both samplers have large areas of unworked canvas and are not of very skilled workmanship.

Children occasionally made a Berlin wool sampler and a Berlin wool picture while at a state school. The two samplers above are really a combination of these two kinds of work—the centre design

52

22 Belgian sampler on double canvas in Berlin wool; mid nineteenth century *The National Museum of Wales, Welsh Folk Museum*

from a picture and the border from a sampler. A sampler at St Fagan's Museum, Cardiff, has a little motif of Penrhyn Castle on it and a picture in needlework using the same design is in their collection. Also in their collection is a picture of a Madonna and Child worked about 1852 by a girl at Miss Pritchard's School, Abergavenny. The design is an unusual one and may not have been taken from a printed pattern. It is worked unevenly in wool and cotton with a predominance of blue.

Fortunately, it was fashionable to include the name and age of the child when their pictures were framed, occasionally the date was also added. Most children's pictures, worked in their early teens, were large and worked on a coarse canvas and animals were a favourite subject. An attractive example seen at Worthing, Sussex, was of a boy dressed in blue with a large parrot and written on the frame was 'Lucinda Matthews worked this in her thirteenth year'. Another seen in Exeter, Devon, was a very large copy of *The Last Supper* worked with a large stitch in crude colours. On the wide wooden frame was written *Sarah Mills aged 13, 1872*.

There are very few map samplers in Berlin wool, as by the time Berlin work was popular map samplers were old fashioned. An interesting one, in a private collection, is of the British Isles, 457 mm × 558 mm (18 in. × 22 in.), worked in 1881 by Ellen Hobart, aged 11. The pattern was printed in black and white by F. Pitman, 20 Paternoster Row, London, and is entitled *Marking Map for Girls' Schools*, No. 2, price 9d. The map of Ireland, illustrated 457 mm × 380 mm (18 in. × 15 in.) is very unusual and a skilled piece of work. The counties are well shaded in fine petit point and the sea is worked in long stitches in an irregular pattern. It was probably made about 1850.

A map sampler worked in Merionieth, at St Fagan's Museum, Cardiff, is 600 mm × 762 mm (24 in. × 30 in.). It is an accurate map of England, Wales and part of Ireland worked with red wool but the wool was too thick for the canvas and was obviously difficult to use, the English Channel and German Ocean (now the North Sea) were named in full but only the initials of the counties were worked.

There are more children's samplers made in Berlin wool in Welsh museums than English ones, but it is not possible to decide if this is because more were made. It may be a great number are still in private homes in England, and certainly the very simple ABC samplers made in some English schools are so small and uninteresting that they are hardly 'museum' pieces.

Berlin pattern samplers were made by needlewomen in the nineteenth century and are true examples of stitches. They are most interesting to study. Apart from the late eighteenth century darning samplers, no similar work had been attempted by adults for over a century, but when it became necessary to have one's own record of stitches for reference, the real sampler came into its own once more. Although many of the little patterns and motifs could be obtained in printed form it was much easier to have a worked example from which to make a choice.

Some of these samplers were embroidered by professionals to be

23　Child's sampler on double canvas in Berlin wool; late nineteenth
century　(page 52)

sold in the fancy work shops or to be kept in the shop for reference to enable the customer to get ideas. Others must have been made by the enthusiast embroideress herself and kept in her work basket, and as new patterns were published they could be added to the canvas. Several long samplers have a length of canvas unworked at one end, others have the designs closer together at one end and better positioned at the other.

The best of these samplers are of great length, usually worked on a single fine white canvas in a variety of wools, silks and beads and they are bound with ribbon, invariably blue, red or black. They are to be found in all parts of the country, but there are not as many as one would imagine there have been. This may be due to the habit of keeping them in a work box or on a shop counter and when they became worn and tatty they were discarded. Of those which have survived the ones in the best condition have been stored in a roll and fastened with a button or ribbon, others have been made into a book, with each canvas 'page' bound with ribbon before being fixed together.

The sampler illustrated is in the author's collection and is quite 20 magnificent. It is 203 mm wide and 488 cm long (8 in. wide and 16 ft long) the last 660 mm (26 in.) is unworked and protects the wool work when the sampler is rolled up. The canvas is white, 22 threads to the inch and bound with blue ribbon. There are over one hundred and seventy designs—borders, corners, flowers, geometrical patterns, florentine patterns, two aphabets and numerous interesting motifs. Several of the motifs appear on other samplers—the fox mask on the top left of the picture is frequently used, always identical; the tassels which are upside-down on the right hand strip are in red. Some samplers have them worked in blue (the tassel design has been used with a background of white beads in the edging for the table cover illustrated). It is surprising that no example of canvas lace work has been included as it often appears on samplers, although rarely on a large piece of work. It was worked with the design in black wool and the background filled with little cross stitches in silk, it must have been very tedious to do and unless it was perfect the effect of imitating lace was lost (diagram i).

A copper kettle can be seen, they were usually embroidered onto kettle holders or tea pot stands shown in diagram ii.

A very attractive tabby cat is sitting on a tuffett of grass. It is much more like a cat than most Victorian representations, they did not seem to be able to portray the appearance of a cat nearly as well as that of a dog and they are seen much less frequently in pictures.

A sampler similar to this at St Fagan's Museum has several of the

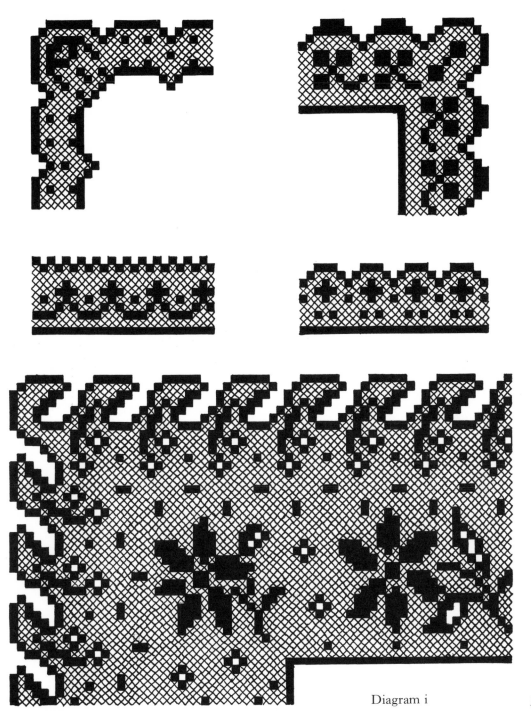

Diagram i

57

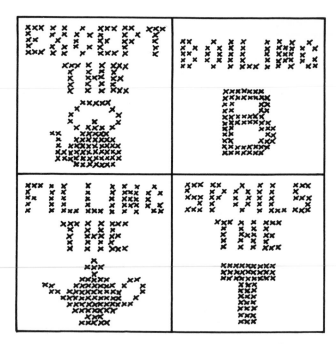

OR

Diagram ii

same motifs included and also a very pretty bird, which is unusual on a sampler. Neither sampler is dated.

It was not usual to sign or date any of these samplers, but they were probably worked between 1835 and 1870. Before 1835 patterns were not easily obtainable for copying, and after 1870 different styles of needlework were becoming fashionable. One dated example is in Brecon Museum, Wales, with 'Patterns 1840' worked in red wool. It has an assortment of little patterns and some florentine work in a variety of colours, but the work looks very shabby and must have had a lot of handling. A dated sampler in the Victoria and Albert Museum was made in 1850 and worked entirely with floral motifs and borders.

Another sampler in the Victoria and Albert Museum is 102 mm wide and 304 cm long (4 in. wide and 10 ft long). It is of very fine workmanship which suggests a professional worker. The designs are arranged to fill the spaces attractively with just sufficient repetition to look pleasant and be suitable for using as a pattern. Wools, silks, beads and silver thread have been used.

As well as these long samplers, other pieces of work for reference were made, but purely for use and not to be attractive to look at. On these the canvas is not bound, the patterns are not completed and sometimes the same pattern has been partly worked several times with different colour combinations. The simplest of these are just practice pieces by a lady who was going to embroider something and has not quite made up her mind what to do. A tiny scrap in St Fagan's Museum has a Berlin pattern made with wool and strips of plaited straw, similar to the kind used in millinery, it is quite unique and one wonders if anything came from the idea; another in the author's collection has a similar pattern with strips of satin ribbon and shades of fawn wool worked on a German cotton canvas.

A piece of canvas with several designs on it was found on a market stall amongst a collection of various oddments of embroidery in a plastic bag. They had been worked at a needlework school at Henley-on-Thames and included hand-made patterns on squared paper and photographs of needlework at the Victoria and Albert Museum. They might have belonged to a teacher but the standard of sewing suggests a pupil. It is difficult to date the work but the Berlin sampler appears older than the rest. On it are a kettle, a fox's mask, canvas lace work and some stitches giving a three dimensional effect.

The last group of samplers belonged either to teachers or, much more likely, to professional embroiderers who sewed for a living. Sewing was an acceptable occupation for a girl who had been unable to get married or had fallen on hard times. Although any form of employment in early Victorian days did lower one in the eyes of society, sewing was not as disreputable as some work. Ladies who were not good needlewomen could order new covers for chairs or stools to be worked for them, or an attractive pelmet to match the fashionable wall paper in a newly decorated room. Upholstered furniture would need re-covering at least every thirty years and this is proved by often finding several layers of material from successive re-coverings on Victorian chairs today. The needlewomen would have worked in their own homes or at the back of a shop and have had a range of canvas wool, silk and patterns for their customers to look at. They would also work designs to order from paper patterns which were supplied by a shop or private individuals. A collection of such samplers (see figure 21, page 51) were found among a collection of old linen in a second hand shop. There are twenty two pieces of canvas, varying from a coarse double canvas with seven threads to the inch with a design of interlocking diamonds in vivid colours, to a very fine single canvas, twenty-nine threads to the inch with a delicate floral band in pastel shades. The thickness of the wool was carefully chosen to suit the canvas and some silk highlights had been used. The workmanship is of the highest standard. Most of the designs are repeating ones, suitable for upholstery but there are a few individual flowers—a rose bud, a convolvulus and a pansy. There is a piece of canvas lace work and a curious paisley type of pattern in multi-colours.

An interesting pattern is pinned to one piece of canvas. It is a tiny, rough, water colour painting, on white paper, of the finished work, which was to have been a square of 120 stitches along the diagonal (this was written on the painting). It is a pattern of black fleur-de-lis, stars and simple flowers on various coloured backgrounds, red, green and blue outlined in yellow. The canvas was sufficiently worked to show the number of stitches required, one fleur-de-lis on a red square, a flower on an outlined square and two stars. It is rare to find an original Berlin pattern hand painted in this way. There is one in the large collection of patterns at the Victoria and Albert Museum which was drawn and painted on white paper and then a grid of squares was drawn in ink afterwards. It has a design of flowers and no attempt had been made to adapt it to the squares.

A similar collection of pieces of canvas with various patterns is in Maidstone Museum, Kent.

It was a great pity that more of the interesting stitches and patterns found on the Berlin samplers were not used on larger pieces of complete work; if they had been, maybe Berlin wool would not have been so despised by the end of the nineteenth century.

5 Furniture

Ever since comfortable chairs were introduced into homes they have been ornamented by hand embroidered covers. In the seventeenth and eighteenth centuries fine canvas work was made by the wealthy upper classes and many beautiful examples of it are still with us today. This work was produced from a design, or at least an outline, drawn in paint or ink onto the canvas and it was worked with strong worsted threads or silk, usually in *petit point,* in a lovely range of colours.

Regency

Berlin patterns were available in this country early in the nineteenth century, but there is very little evidence that they were used in any quantity for upholstered furniture before 1830. During the period 1800–1830, known as the Regency, designs of chairs and sofas were not really suited to the small Berlin patterns that were being imported. Most pieces of needlework that were made for furniture at this time were probably worked in wool or silk using a design drawn onto the canvas, in the same way as late eighteenth century work, although on a few chairs and stools Berlin patterns may have been used.

The Regency sofa and *chaise-longue* were hard and uncomfortable, for springs were not invented until 1850, and they were not improved by the fashion for solid, cylindrical sofa-pillows, often in Berlin work, adorned with a tassel, which was placed at one or both ends. These pillows remained popular until the early 1870s and instructions for making them were published regularly in magazines.

Another piece of Regency furniture that could be decorated with a Berlin pattern was the long, low ottoman seat without back or sides. The top was sometimes hinged so that the inside could be used for storage, but this was more usual with later pieces when they became very popular. There was also a very different circular seat called an ottoman, with backs which allowed sitters on opposite sides or all round. This ottoman was rarely covered with needlework but may have had Berlin cushions, round or square, which were stuffed with feathers. They were only found in very large houses.

Regency pole screens were nearly all embroidered with silks on silk, or with delicate designs in wools on canvas. A very few may have been decorated using Berlin patterns, but the Regency screens with a design worked in Berlin wools have probably been added later, to replace an older piece which was worn. The needlework was either mounted on a square, shield-shaped, or oval frame and often protected by glass, and this could be raised or lowered to protect ones face from the fire. The design of the pole and base may help to date the needlework—those with tripod legs are very early, later Regency designs have a solid wooden base. At The Pavilion, Brighton, there is a screen dated 1810, which has a delicate floral pattern worked with Berlin wool and other threads. When pole screens became unfashionable, the needlework was sometimes retained when the pole was discarded, and there are many of these framed panels posing as pictures. On a Regency pole screen it is unlikely to find the needlework with a worked background as the fine silk canvas that was popular did not require covering all over.

Small face screens were made from Berlin patterns but it is very difficult to tell the difference between Regency and early Victorian ones, and this applies to stools as well.

Victorian

Berlin wool work was so popular in early Victorian times that it was synonymous with embroidery. It continued to be made during the whole century for furniture and decorative trifles for the home, only very gradually giving way to the ideas of the Arts and Craft Movement and the designs of men such as William Morris.

Patterns for Berlin work for furniture had a good sale in the shops throughout Victoria's reign, but most magazines ceased to produce them regularly after the 1870s. With the wealth of designs being published just after the Great Exhibition, it is almost incredible to find a book produced in the early sixties suggesting that Berlin work had become unfashionable. *The Illustrated Girl's Own Treasury* noted that 'since the introduction of raised or plush work, Berlin work had re-asserted itself after many years of little or none of it being done'. With a statement like this, one wondered wherever the writer had been. Nothing like the craze for Berlin work had ever existed before Victorian times and there has been nothing quite like it since. There could have been hardly an upper or middle class home in the land without a piece of the work in 1860.

The invention of the railway in 1830 influenced the popularity of Berlin work and designs in general. As people travelled more quickly and easily from London to the provinces, new ideas swept the country, helped by the great increase of cheap publications. Previously new ideas in fashion, furniture and architecture had taken many years to filter through, but now provincial towns became as fashionable as London.

About 1830, the making of furniture in classical style, gave way to revivals of Gothic and Elizabethan designs and these well-padded shapes were perfect for the new fashion in needlework. One style known as *Abbotsford* after the influence of Sir Walter Scott's romantic stories was particularly popular for thirty years. Scott was extraordinarily successful in his life time and highly regarded.

The furnishings in the various rooms in a house were divided between 'his' being predominately comfortable in the dining room, library, study and smoking room with dark, serviceable, leather or velvet fabrics and 'hers' which showed a lady's desire for elegance in the delicate fabrics and floral needlework of the drawing room and bedrooms. In a magazine of 1870, a design for a rug in stripes is described as 'a severe style fit for a study or library'.

Most of the needlework made for furniture was a leisure-time pursuit of the ladies of the house, but some was done professionally. Either type of work looked much better if it was mounted properly by upholsterers or furniture makers who advertized for work in magazines and papers.

Hygienic stuffings were used at home as the instruction for making a sofa pillow show in 1867 'Five pounds of poultry feathers should be dried well by tying in paper bags and putting them in the oven for six nights after the fire has gone out', but the stuffings used in the trade were not always of such a high standard.

In September 1849 *The Art Journal* carried this notice 'Ladies may have their work made up into a variety of elegant articles such as chairs, ottomans, footstools—from £2 upwards, J. B. Robinson, Wood carver, Belpar, Derbyshire'. During that year mahogany dining room chairs were advertised at 14s 0d and drawing room chairs at 16s 6d. Two years later Williams Fashionable Upholstery Warehouse, Portman Square, London, advertised that they had pieces of handsome needlework for sale at 2s 6d, devotional chairs at £1 1s 0d and ottomans at 7s 6d.

A glance through furniture-makers pattern books at the time when Berlin work was at its height, will show many illustrations of the use of needlework on upholstery and there was at least one designer who produced a book especially for this, Henry Wood's *A Useful and Modern Work on Cheval and Pole Screens, Ottomans, Chairs and Settees for Mounting Berlin Needlework* published in 1845. The eighteen plates include the most elaborate and extraordinary designs for furniture in all the most popular styles of the day, including several *prie dieu* chairs, very ornate screens and chairs with carved woodwork. No attempt had been made by him to choose suitable needlework for his designs, they were nearly all covered with similar floral patterns.

It would be easy if one could date needlework accurately by the furniture it was on. Of course, this gives a good indication of when it might have been made, but it is in no way completely reliable. It is possible to date furniture very exactly, often to within ten years, but the fashions in Berlin work were not only dictated by the pattern designers and magazines, they were greatly influenced by personal taste. However, a study of the most popular designs associated with each style will help, and it is also worth remembering that the needlework is invariably less old than the piece of furniture and will certainly not precede it. The condition of the needlework is not a pointer to its age, only how carefully it has been looked after; some pieces made for chairs before the middle of the century have had loose covers for most of their life and are in better condition than others which were made in the 1890s.

A simple method of dating which is, nevertheless, fairly accurate is to remember the dates for the fashionable background colours.

Before 1850, the groundings were pale delicate, pastel colours, light and gay; which were the perfect foil for the moss roses, cornflowers and carnations (the latter had always been a popular flower since the days of the Jacobites). Most needlework with unworked backgrounds fit into this period.

With the 1860s came backgrounds of black, vivid blue and red made with the new aniline dyes. The designs included many new flowers that were being grown in conservatories such as gloxinias, fuchsias, amaryllis and tiger lilies, also vivid cabbage roses, madonna lilies and auriculas. The living rooms of mid-Victorian times were certainly not as dull and dark as some modern authors and playwrights would lead us to believe. The colours were brilliant, with beautiful wallpaper, rich carpets and fabulous colour in the clothes of the ladies and gentlemen. One hundred years of wear and tear has left everything muted and subdued, especially Berlin wool work, and it is only when one finds something which has spent the years behind cupboard doors that one realised the wealth of colour that was in their homes.

The designs of the 1870s favoured the browns, greens and dull crimsons, with geometric patterns and scrolls.

The various colours which predominate in certain periods were complementary to other furnishing of that time, and a study of the fashionable textiles, carpets or wallpaper will confirm this.

Chairs

The *prie dieu* or devotional chair was an original design of the 26 nineteenth century and was often covered with needlework. It was not, as some assume, only meant for private prayers, although those in High Church households were used for this purpose and were decorated accordingly with 'suitable' designs—gothic tracery, crosses, passion flowers or cherubs.

24 Early Victorian chair in cross stitch and
raised wool work; light coloured grounding

25 Mid-Victorian chair with wool and bead embroidery; dark coloured grounding *The National Museum of Wales, Welsh Folk Museum*

The tall-backed chairs were often made in *Abbotsford* style with
26 barley-sugar twist legs in antiqued blackened wood. They always had
a flat upholstered surface on the top of the back. Those with a T-
shaped top surrounded with a wooden edge are not really *prie dieus*.
The earliest examples made in the thirties were usually covered in
dark velvet but by the fifties needlework was very common and the
carving had become more elaborate. They went out of fashion about
1870, but before this some very cheap copies were made with poor
quality workmanship to satisfy the demands for a popular chair.

The majority of suitable needlework patterns had the design
adapted to the shape of the chair. Those which tried to imitate the
Gothic architecture of the time and mix it with religious symbols,
showed a complete lack of feeling for beauty in design and some
disastrous attempts can be found. In the Victoria and Albert Museum
is a pattern for a *prie dieu* chair published by L. W. Wittich, Berlin,
with a chalice and passion flowers included in the hand coloured
design, it was used in 1835. The designs incorporating familiar
flowers were the most popular, especially roses climbing up the back
or in a bunch or garland. Critics of Berlin work either complained
that flowers were unsuitable on a devotional chair or that religious
symbols suggested Popery. Obviously it was not possible to please
everyone and from the large number of designs available, one just
embroidered one's personal choice.

The method of dating needlework by the background colour is
possible with the floral patterns, but most religious ones are probably
pre-1855. Coats of arms are sometimes seen on these chairs, both
carved and in needlework. They are usually faked, except those on
the chairs of highest quality. Berlin designs with scrolls or repeated
geometric shapes were successful and attractive on this design of chair.

Another type of chair which was suitable for Berlin wool work was
the sewing or low chair. This chair had a continuous seat and back
with no arms; it came into fashion at the end of the Regency period
and was popular for fifty years. The earliest ones were light and
graceful, with squat cabriole legs which were sometimes carved on
the knees, and they were made of rosewood, walnut or ebonized and
gilded. By 1860 the design had become heavier and over-padded but
they were still a very popular chair for the ladies with their volumin-
ous skirts. They are sometimes called ladies chairs, but are not
nursing chairs—these always had a washable cover. Some sewing
chairs have the most delightful designs in needlework, worked on a
fine canvas, with flowers such as roses or lilies or attractive foliage on
a pastel ground.

These chairs could be ornamented in a different way by having them covered entirely in furnishing satin or velvet and then adding a continuous strip of needlework about six inches wide down the centre of the back and seat. These strips are sometimes confused with bell pulls if they have been removed from the chair, as similar repeating patterns were used on both. A low chair seen in Exeter, Devon, was entirely covered in black satin and buttoned; the slender black and gold frame was probably made about 1840 but the strip of needlework was much later and rather unattractive with a design in fawns and magenta, reminiscent of the garish tiles around a late-Victorian fireplace.

Patterns specially shaped to fit the seats and backs of chairs could be bought in all the popular designs. The one illustrated is hand 8 painted in shades of yellow and browns on a blue background. The patterns issued with magazines were not usually shaped and the worker adapted the design to fit by working the background the correct size.

Bergere chairs in beech, elm or pine with high backs and low seats were decorated with floral needlework from the mid-century. Louis chairs, copies of French designs, with upholstered back, seat and arms, which were often made specially for customers, favoured patterns that were small and repeated, although large flowers were used as well. A grandfather chair dates from about 1840 and had wooden arms, a lady's low chair and occasionally a *chaise-longue* could be made to match and are sometimes seen with needlework covers.

Balloon back chairs, in all their variations, were made in sets. The elegant drawing room and bedroom chairs looked delightful with embroidered seats. Unfortunately the designs which were chosen did not always harmonise with the frame and a pretty chair could be quite spoilt. For example, a chair about 1850 which had been covered with a design of large bright peacock feathers and roses in green, blue, yellow and white on a vivid red background.

When embroidering a set of chair seats, it was possible to buy a set of patterns with similar but not identical designs. Designs in pairs for chair seats were given away at Christmas time in some magazines.

A mention must be made of *papier mâché* furniture. Chairs made of this material with needlework upholstery date from about 1840 but are not common. Designs with brilliant exotic flowers or tropical birds suited this style of chair better than floral wreaths and bouquets.

Although wool was the most usual medium to use on chairs, beads are to be found either used for grounding, for the whole design, or just for the highlights. A rather splendid pair of chairs had a picture of Queen Victoria and Prince Albert worked entirely in beads on them;

26 *Prie dieu* chair with wool and bead embroidery, *c.* 1870   *The National Museum of Wales, Welsh Folk Museum*

the pattern was probably taken from a Baxter print and was no doubt worked at a similar time to the pair in the Victoria and Albert Museum with painted portraits which were made for the Great Exhibition. The *prie dieu* chair illustrated has some beadwork on it. 26

Berlin patterns on chairs embroidered wholly in silk or with silk backgrounds must have been very beautiful when they were new, but in the few remaining examples today the condition of the silk nearly always spoils the appearance. A beautiful piece of work of French origin at the Victoria and Albert Museum has a floral design of wool and a grounding of silk. French designs for Berlin work have a delicacy about them missing from most German and English ones, and this chair seat is particularly attractive although not in pristine condition.

Sofas and the chaise-longue

The *chaise-longue* was a single-ended piece of furniture that had taken the place of the day bed. It was very fashionable throughout the nineteenth century. The earlier ones were very elegant with carved cabriole legs, but in accordance with all types of furniture they became heavier and less attractive as the century progressed. Walnut, rosewood or mahogany ones would sometimes be made to match a set of drawing or dining room chairs. They were seldom covered completely in needlework but had Berlin cushions as in Regency times.

The Victorian sofa, settee or chesterfield is a more massive piece of furniture and well padded. The illustration of the settee covered in 27 squares of needlework is an amazing example, the date of 1845 is worked into one square, with a picture of a hussar. It was worked by Lady Mary Hamlyn-Williams and her friends of Edwinsford, a large mansion in Carmarthenshire, Wales, and is now in St Fagan's Museum, Cardiff. It is 239 cm long, 76 cm deep and 94 cm high (7 ft 10 in. long, 2 ft 6 in. deep and 3 ft 1 in. high). It formed part of the furnishings of the drawing room in which the chairs, footstools, cushions, screen and window drapes were all in Berlin work. It must be unique and although not a work of art, it is quite fascinating and must have amused countless visitors. Several of the squares have well-known motifs—the little King Charles Spaniel on a cushion, the Prince of Wales feathers, (favourites on slippers), butterflies, the fox's mask and the witch on her broomstick. Some are complicated patterns worked with a very small stitch.

Another sofa, about 1870, which is very large and well stuffed with horse-hair has a much plainer design than the Welsh one and is covered with a repeating design of large overblown roses on a bright yellow background. The colour of this grounding does not correspond to the usual choice for this period.

27 Settee 238 cm (7 ft 10 in.) long from Edwinsford, Carmarthenshire 1845; it formed part of the furnishings of the drawing room and was accompanied by chairs, stools, cushions, screens and curtains all embroidered in Berlin wool by the family   *The National Museum of Wales, Welsh Folk Museum*

28 Settee 183 cm (6 ft) long; roses and fuchsias on a yellow ground. Mid-Victorian   *Mrs Violet Wood*

The ottoman, in both its forms, was used throughout this period, but it was not a favourite item for the needlewoman. The circular type would have been particularly difficult to work.

Footstools

It was considered necessary to have a footstool for each chair and some spares. They vary in size and shape considerably and some were made to follow the pattern of the legs of the chairs or sofa. They were frequently embroidered with wool, beads or a mixture of both.

Small stools made about 1835 had low cabriole legs and were usually covered with floral patterns. About 1850 a small round stool was made with china feet, and beadwork tops were common with flowers, animals, birds or little strapwork patterns. During the late sixties most stools had wooden surrounds with similar patterns, together with some attractive three-dimensional designs. After this date, there were many individual designs made.

A different type of stool was the long, low one to be placed by the fender. It had nicely shaped legs and was sometimes made to slope away from the fire. Some of these stools have beautiful needlework designs. Naturalistic roses and lilies on a vivid background in wool or beadwork are often seen and strapwork designs with a blue grounding all in beads were particularly fashionable.

Very unusual stools are seen occasionally such as the Hour-Glass stool which speaks for itself and is more of a seat than a footstool and a three legged piano stool made in a rustic effect. One illustration in *The Graphic* 1883 contained a 'genteel spittoon', the upholstered top could be hinged up to reveal a porcelain or metal container; the octagonal walnut variety cost 6s 9d, the round one in mahogany, walnut or ebonised 9s 6d. An 'elliptic footstool' of a most strange shape was illustrated in the *Englishwoman's Domestic Magazine* 1864; it cost 7s 6d and 3s 8d for the embroidery materials.

Patterns for round music stools were invariably floral wreaths and were often given away in magazines to be used for this or on round cushions. Although some very delicate designs were made, one given away in 1870 was quite startling, with leaves and stars in scarlet, violet, green, brown, gold, white and blue.

Some stools were made with Tunbridge Ware frames, this was a wood mosiac built up from different coloured woods into a pattern. Each slender strip of wood was square in section and these were glued together in a bundle in a definite pattern. This was then sliced across the bundle and the identical veneers would be mounted onto solid pine, beech or rosewood. Each veneer was an exact copy of the original

29   Stools. The square one has a tile pattern design, *c.* 1845; the curved
stool is one of a pair and the octagonal shape contains a spittoon. A spittoon
of similar design was advertised for 6s 9d during 1870   *Mrs Violet Wood*

30   Fender stool *c.* 1850   *Mrs Violet Wood*

pattern. Although Tunbridge Ware was made in the eighteenth century there was much more produced after 1830 and many of the designs used by the craftsmen were actual Berlin wool patterns—floral wreaths, borders and all the popular motifs found in needlework can be found in Tunbridge Ware, even quite complicated pictorial subjects. The Museum at Tunbridge Wells has an excellent collection of the ware including a reconstruction of a workshop and some of the Berlin patterns that were used.

Berlin patterns were used for a similar type of work using wool instead of wood, it was known as mosaic work and produced pictures in a kind of plush. There are directions for doing this by hand in the *Dictionary of Needlework* and it was made commercially from about 1840–1870 by John Crossley & Sons of Halifax, under the name of *Crossley Mosaics,* and by other firms in France and America. Although the pictures were not necessarily made from actual Berlin patterns, they were built up in squares in a similar way. The woollen threads were laid in exactly the same way as the strips of wood in Tunbridge Ware and kept in place by wood and wires until they were glued; then slices were stuck to linen and cut off. Hundreds could be cut from one laying, but towards the end of the run, the design was often distorted.

There was much criticism about the choice of needlework designs on furniture and Mrs Merrifield wrote a long article about it in the *Art Journal* 1853.

'Ladies delight above all with direct imitation of nature in all the art forms. A pretty bird, a soft eyed animal or a gigantic specimen of the exotic flower is greeted by 'How natural' and the pattern is bought to adorn a footstool or firescreen. No flower, bird or animal should be used to be trodden underfoot and to so so violates the rules of ornamental design. If ladies gave some thought to suitable design, there are good Berlin patterns to be selected. The practice of selling patterns to be returned and resold after use is in the favour of the trade but not in the improvement of designs. Of course there are always those who will buy the cheapest even by a few pence and frequently the cheapest pattern has an indifferent design and is chosen because of the price. Good, expensive patterns could be lent on subscription as in the case of drawings and books.' (Later on, several magazines ran exchange columns where items, including Berlin patterns could be exchanged. In America the exchanging of patterns was done by friendly arrangement in ladies circles such as those organised by their church.) There is definitely an attitude at this time among ladies working for leisure that while time is unlimited, thought must be at a minimum.

The bad choice of use of design is seen in the use of the popular

Prince of Wales in sailor suit. When used on a footstool, he is seen, not standing as the designer intended, but lying on his back looking upwards. This is not only contrary to nature, but also an indignity, as to put one's foot on the stool represents the defeat of the enemy. To put roses or lilies on a stool means that they will be crumpled underfoot. Another stool top I have seen, had a sort of Gothic architectural pattern in relief in imitation of gold; in this were worked at intervals, imitation gems with lights, shades and reflections. The centre was occupied by an imitation in colour of the flowers and leaves of the arum. It is just bad taste.'

Screens
Designs with much detail were considered suitable on cheval screens for summer use and favourites were copies of well known paintings such as Landseer's *Bolton Abbey in Olden Time, The Monarch of the Glen* or pictures illustrating scenes from popular novels of the time, especially Sir Walter Scott's books. Engravings of such pictures were published regularly in many magazines and were very well known. Oversized tropical birds and pet animals were also popular.

32

There is an interesting firescreen belonging to the Queen of *Islay and Tilco with a Red Macaw and Two Lovebirds*. The wood is less heavy than on some screens and carved with twisted uprights. Landseer painted the original picture for Victoria in 1839 and it was placed in the drawing room at Osborne. Islay was the Queen's favourite Sky Terrier who died on 26 April 1839. The Prince Consort broke the news to her and she wrote 'the sad news that my faithful little companion for more than five years is no more. I was much shocked and distressed'. She had previously told her uncle, Leopold I, that 'my little Scotch dog is always with me and he is a great darling, but a cat bit him poor fellow'. The original painting 1120 mm × 686 mm (50 in. × 27 in.) was exhibited at the Royal Academy in 1840 and a copy was made from it for the Berlin picture. This is different from the original in several places and different yet again from another needlework copy of the same size bought in Australia and now in the collection of Mrs Humphrey Brand of Glydne, Sussex. The painting has a very plain background suggesting the corner of a room, with floor, skirting board and plain walls. The firescreen belonging to the Queen has the animals and birds in the same positions but outdoors, with roses, bushes, trees and a castle. The one belonging to Mrs Brand is elaborated still further with the same roses in the foreground but with trees and hills going away into the distance, that nearly fill the canvas.

It was not unusual to alter the background and details when making a needlework pattern from a painting and the Countess of Wilton in her book remarks on it and says how these alterations spoil the whole mood of the painting.

In this case, it is interesting to wonder if the Queen's needlework picture was specially painted for her and was not the same pattern issued in the Berlin Wool Repositories?

Another Landseer picture of a macaw and a basket of flowers is in Mrs Brand's collection and a copy of this was also a firescreen belonging to the Royal Family. This is now in the Victoria and Albert Museum. An interesting needlework picture about 610 mm × 686 mm (24 in. × 27 in.), also in Mrs Brand's collection, is of a woman looking through the window of a house at a little girl reading with her pet dog. In the empty grate stands a cheval screen with a Berlin picture upon it.

A most peculiar and unattractive pattern for a cheval screen was given away with the *Young Ladies Journal* in 1882—it typifies the very worst in design. It is entitled *The Knight and The Lady* and has a strange gentleman holding a standard, cap in hand gazing at a maiden squashed into the top right hand corner of the picture and presumably inside a building; between them is an enormous pot containing trailing plants and in the distance is a castle. At the bottom is given particulars of obtaining materials and also a deal hand frame for working the design for 1s 9d. The suppliers undertake to mount the work; it is 370 mm × 230 mm (14½ in. × 13 in.) in an elegant brass cheval screen for 38s 6d. It is not uncommon to find pictorial subjects that were given away with magazines of particularly bad design.

For winter use, the pole screen was used. During the early part of Victoria's reign designs were similar to those during Regency times, with a circular wooden base to the pole, but gradually the banner screen became fashionable and by 1870 it was almost universal. The banner was hung from a wooden or metal crossbar.

There were innumerable patterns produced for banner screens and from the dated examples given away with magazines it appears that floral designs gave way to very popular geometrical shapes after 1865, although there were plenty of flowers used later than this. The February edition of the *Young Ladies Journal* 1870 had a coloured banner design with roses and other flowers; a note added that J. Bedford and Company of Regent Street and Tottenham Court Road, London, could supply the materials with either imitation silk canvas (German) or Penelope canvas at 4s 9d or with silk for the high-lights at 1s 6d extra—post free for 81 stamps.

Some of the nicest designs were worked completely with beads or with beads on a silk or wool background, from about 1855. They often have silk or bead fringes. In the collection of Mr C. F. Colt at Bethersden, Kent, are several beautiful examples now used as wall decorations and cushions, among which are some of exceptional interest. A pair of cushions made from banners have a silk background on which a bouquet of flowers is worked most expertly. The design is very artistic and unusual and is probably the work of a gifted amateur artist and not copied from a commercial pattern. A banner with a design of roses and anemones in brilliant colours has an 37 unusual lace effect around the edge produced with white beads.

31 Cheval screen *The Sicilian Maid* from Glamorgan, Wales. Mid-Victorian *The National Museum of Wales Folk Museum* (page 109)

Banners with the design in white, grey and steel beads were attractive before 1870, especially those with brilliant wool backgrounds, but about this time some crude patterns worked with fairly coarse beads were made and these heralded the last of the banner designs.

There is a banner made in memory of the Prince Consort in the Victoria and Albert Museum. It has a background of blue wool on which is a border of roses and in the centre is a medallion, draped with a cloth, on which has been worked in silks and steel, white and grey beads. *To the Memory of Albert, Prince Consort d. 1861*. It is unusual to find a memorial banner, but there were framed pictures made in memory of a dear one. The illustration of the memorial to a young 58 girl shows clearly how the working of the *petit point* stitch backwards and forwards at the bottom has pulled the canvas out of shape, although it stayed straight at the top where it was correctly worked across the diagonal. Memorials were predominately black and white, very personal and very sad.

32 Cheval screen *Bolton Abbey in Olden Time c. 1845 Mrs Humphrey Brand* (page 75).

Miniature banner screens, usually in pairs about 305 mm (12 in.) high were made to shield one's face from the fire. The stems were metal, white china or ivory and the needlework was very similar to that on the large screens, beadwork being particularly popular. Small hand screens, usually circular and fringed (see figure 33) continued to be made in similar designs to those of the Regency.

A delightful doll's house in Wells Museum, Somerset, has an enchanting wooden polescreen about 64 mm (2½ in.) high in the drawing room with a minute design of roses from a Berlin pattern.

Another type of screen, in the form of a banner hanging from an adjustable metal bracket, could be fixed to the wall near the fire and pulled into position when it was needed. It was a Victorian invention and most of them were made during the second half of the century. There is one in the Bath Museum of Costume dated about 1857 with a pattern of grey and white beads on a red woollen background which has an attractive lace effect as a border worked with cream beads.

33 Pair of hand screens worked with fine Berlin wool on silk canvas; grounding unworked, *c.* 1835 *Maidstone Museum*

80   34   Panel for a cheval screen *c.* 1850   *Mrs Violet Wood*

35   Banner screen in beads and silk *c.* 1870   *Miss Edna M. Cole*

36   Pole screen in wool with grounding unworked; pole of gilded metal
c. 1850   *Rochester Museum*

37   Banner screen in beads and wool with the lace edging worked with
beads; brilliant colours   *Mr C. F. Colt*

References to screens in American books show that very similar designs were in use there. In 1850 a book published in New York *The Architecture of Country Houses,* gave illustrations of an elaborately carved mahogany cheval screen for the parlour, a banner pole screen for the drawing room and two pole screens with needlework behind glass, also for the drawing room, one circular and the other rectangular.

Cushions

38   Cushion on jute canvas with beads and raised wool work; grounding unworked *c.* 1850   *Mrs Humphrey Brand*

39　Coat of Arms on cushion with brown ground 1860
Mrs Humphrey Brand

40　Edge from a table cover; tassels in wool, grounding in white beads
c. 1860
41　Pair of bell pulls in wool with oak leaves on a dark red ground　*The* ▶
National Museum of Wales, Welsh Folk Museum

Carpets

Carpets and rugs were made of Berlin wool and from Berlin patterns. The majority of them were made in tile patterns; that is, in form of squares which were joined together when complete, although some small pieces were worked in this style but as a whole and not joined. Many of the remaining example have floral motifs and a running floral or leafy border, but geometric designs, animals and various other patterns were used. Most of the tiles were square but diamonds and hexagons were made by the more adventurous workers. Cross stitch, being a hard-wearing stitch was most frequently used and some examples in this stitch have worn very well and are still in use today. A much quicker stitch was Leviathan stitch, in which thick wool made a cross stitch of two vertical and one horizontal thread on a coarse double canvas, but only simple patterns were possible.

Probably the largest Berlin carpet ever made was exhibited at the Great Exhibition and described in that chapter, but there are two fairly large carpets at the Victoria and Albert Museum. One was worked about 1840 to 1850 in Berlin wools on linen, it measures 488 cm × 366 cm (16 ft × 12 ft) and is made up of square tiles 60 cm × 60 cm (2 ft × 2 ft) with a variety of floral and geometric designs and a floral border, all worked in cross stitch. The other carpet measures 366 cm × 244 cm (12 ft × 8 ft) and was worked in one piece in a much coarser stitch with designs of floral motifs in medallions. Both these carpets are in good condition.

Patterns for rugs were occasionally given away in magazines. A rug in the Bath Museum of Costume dated about 1880 has an easy repeating pattern similar to those found in the journals, but the colours, red and pink, are unusual; the ends are finished with hand made tassels. This rug is in one of the very interesting period rooms at this museum and in it there is also a dolls house which has miniature Berlin rugs in some of its rooms.

Another type of Berlin carpet or rug was made to imitate Persian and Turkish carpets. The designs were not actual copies but 'anglicized', although the colours were those of the originals—reds, blues, dark greens, black and white. The illustration of such a carpet 42 has the date embroidered, *1844*.

From the vast assortment of Berlin wool work that was used for furniture and furnishing a mention can be made about coats-of-arms. These were very popular and real or fake arms were put onto furniture and framed as pictures. The Victoria and Albert Museum have an interesting collection of armoral patterns printed on cards which include Oriel, Exeter and Worcester Colleges, Oxford and Gonville and Caius and St John's, Cambridge. The Royal Coat of Arms was also available as a Berlin pattern over many years and the worked examples usually had a dark background, either olive green or brown.

The following explanation came from the *Ladies Treasury* 1867, together with a pattern for a table cover to be made as a bridal gift. 'In the centre is a Greek cross, as a marriage based on the power of the cross must, betide what will, be a happy one. The entwined circle beyond the star of leaves is emblematical of the union. The brown tinted portion represents the bridegroom, the scarlet the bride, who should be to him the poetry of life. Each scarlet point rests on an azure ground, strewn with orange flowers for the mother and her offspring—blossom, bud and fruit at once. The brown points touch each other—larger designs significant of man's wider scope to mingle in the world's industry, art and commerce. The whole is surrounded by a band of cornucopias, typical of peace and plenty.'

After this, what more can be said, except to mention how badly paid the professional needlewomen were who undertook to make the ideas given in the magazines, they must have sewn for many hours to earn a shilling. In 1863 a pattern for a toilet cushion was published with the *Englishwoman's Domestic Magazine* together with the cost of the materials from Mrs Wilcockson of London; 1s 11d for the canvas and wools or 8s 5d completely worked.

42   Berlin wool carpet 183 cm × 244 cm (6 ft × 8 ft) 1848   *Mrs Violet Wood*

6 Pictures

There are more examples of Berlin wool pictures surviving than any other forms of this work, but this is to be expected, as it was considered a great accomplishment to work them and something to be carefully preserved, in spite of all the critics had to say. Some have always been behind glass, but even without this, the wool was protected from abrasion, although they were exposed to dirt and moth damage.

Pictorial embroidery has fascinated needlewomen from the earliest times and many interesting aspects of the way people lived and what they enjoyed can be learnt from studying old needlework. Unfortunately the popular designs made from Berlin patterns only show how fashion influenced the subjects and they give very few clues about the ladies who did the work.

The idea of making woolwork imitations of oil paintings started during the late eighteenth century, and the most famous needlewoman at that period was Miss Linwood, who lived from 1755 to 1845. She became so much admired during her life time, that she had a permanent exhibition of her work in Leicester Square, London. Her work was never carried out with Berlin wools but with specially made and dyed worsted threads and she used these on linen, making the design with long stitches guided by the original painting and possibly ink outlines drawn onto the linen. Miss Linwood's work and that of her contemporaries was very skilled and only attempted by a few ladies.

The majority of needlewomen who wanted to make an embroidered picture during the last twenty years of the eighteenth century and up until Berlin patterns became freely available about 1830, made what was known as a 'satin sketch'. This was a design drawn in sepia ink or printed onto cream silk or satin, with the face, hands, feet and sometimes the background painted in water colours. The rest of the figures, trees and other details were added with a needle. It is very noticeable that the painting was often done with greater skill than the sewing. These pictures were produced in very large numbers but few are in perfect condition because the silk, on which they were worked, has discoloured and cracked with age. The earliest examples of satin sketches were pictures of fashionable ladies, pastoral and religious scenes, embroidered with twisted silks and sometimes a little chenille for the trees, but later examples can be found where Berlin wool proved a quick, though not too successful substitute.

Satin sketches were worked with Berlin wool until the mid-century, but by then, they were nearly all Bible stories, although occasionally a small picture with a secular subject is seen. The illustration of *Jesus* 43 *Healing the Blind Man* is Berlin wool on satin. It is well stitched but the composition is a strange mixture of clothes from the Holy Land and very English country scene. Pictures on satin were never made from a Berlin pattern, but it is interesting that there are identical designs worked as satin sketches and as Berlin pictures on canvas, presumably copied from a Berlin pattern. A popular satin sketch was a picture of *Joseph presenting his father to Pharoah,* and the examples worked in Berlin wool have the faces, limbs and the sky painted. Copies of this design on canvas are numerous, including one in the Victoria and Albert Museum dated 1885. Although the proportions vary slightly and one or two details have been altered, both types of needlework are instantly recognisable as copies from the same original painting. It is quite remarkable how very similar the painted and stitched faces are, and how well the colours have been matched.

43 Small satin sketch with the embroidery in Berlin wool; *Christ healing the Blind Man c.* 1830; the surrounding metal braid and red material are original

Another interesting fact about this particular design is that although the artist is unknown, he painted at least one other picture which was made into a Berlin pattern. It was from this painting that the illustration of *Jacob on his death-bed* was taken. The features on Joseph's face are identical in both pictures and they must have been painted by the same artist. There are no doubt many instances where an artist has been responsible for several Berlin patterns, but unless he is well-known as a painter, such as with Landseer, it is pure chance if two examples of his work as needlework pictures come together and can be compared. Just such a stroke of fate brought together a picture of three little girls and one of three choir boys, which as well as being by the same artist, were doubtless the same children made to look like girls in one picture and boys in the other.

Several Berlin pictures were made in pairs and if they are together, it is probably correct to assume they were originally painted by the same artist. The pair of pictures of parrots and their patterns, illustrated, were published with the *Young Ladies Journal* Christmas 1871 and January 1872 and are very similar in style. Incidently, the wool for each parrot could be supplied for 3s 10d and with some silk for highlights 1s 0d extra; a silk fringe and tassels cost 6s 9d and a brass tripod screen to hang it on when complete 27s 6d. They belong to Miss E. M. Cole. Another example of a pair of pictures is in the collection of Mrs Brand at Glynde Place, Sussex. Both designs are of a gamekeeper or a poacher about 305 mm × 457 mm (12 in. × 18 in.). In one he is arriving home and being greeted by his child and dog and in the other he is seated at the table with his boots beside him, his gun put away and his dog feeding from a bowl. They are very detailed pictures and most attractive with the various shades of browns toning with the maple frames. Mrs Brand has another, slightly larger picture of the man at rest, and it would be very easy to accept this on its own and be unaware of its companion, if they were not all together.

The first Berlin patterns were for floral designs and it is not possible to know when the first patterns for pictures appeared. Unless the work is dated, which was not often done, or there is some other reliable evidence, it is difficult to be accurate about the year a picture was made. The patterns for pictures given away with magazines during the second half of the nineteenth century were dated but those produced by the printer to be sold in the shops were only numbered, which does not help much. Of course, there were fashionable subjects and artists at certain times, but personal taste also plays an important part when choosing a picture for one's home. The pattern cannot pre-date the original, but so many of these were the work of little or

11–14

44 Small picture *Jacob on his death bed* in Berlin wool; this is an early pattern and there are copies of the same painting as satin sketches *Mrs Violet Wood*

unknown artists. Popular Berlin patterns were available for as long as fifty years and it would be quite wrong to date one copy by a similar one.

A vital clue for dating a picture may sometimes be found if a search is made behind the frame. The majority of Berlin pictures, as with other pieces of needlework, were nailed or lashed to a stretcher—a rectangular frame or piece of wood. It was the custom to glue paper over the back of the stretcher when the embroidery was in position and when a newspaper or magazine was at hand this was often used. This is not a foolproof method but it seems likely that a fairly recent copy of a periodical would be used rather than one many years old. The colour plate of the parrot in raised wool work had a newspaper dated 1849 on the back which is a very suitable date for the needlework. The oval photograph of the lady, embellished with flowers had been re-framed at some time, as there were traces of a very old paper discussing the building of a railway station at Bristol on land belonging to a Mr Fry (of chocolate fame?); and some pages from a catalogue dated just after the turn of this century.

Needlework was often mounted professionally by picture framers. A trade plate stated 'J. Portus, Carver, Gilder and Picture-Frame Maker, opposite the Gate, Trim Street, Bath. All kinds of glass frames executed in the newest taste. Needlework strained and framed in the neatest manner on reasonable terms'. Also written onto the paper in ink was the date 1855.

The earliest dated examples of Berlin wool pictures appear to be from the 1830s. In the Ulster Museum and Art Gallery there is a picture of a goldfinch dated 1830, and also a copy of *The Last Appeal* a picture of two lovers by a well, dated 1835, (this was used on a Pratt's pot lid several years later).

Mrs Merrifield, in her long criticism of Berlin work in the *Art Journal* 1853, suggested that the idea of copying pictures became fashionable because of the large number of shades available in Berlin wool, but this was not really the reason; the colours just made accurate copying easier. Of all the types of Berlin wool attempted, Mrs Merrifield was most contemptuous of the pictures, 'Barbarous' she called them, making the materials conform to the design instead of the design to the materials. 'We have distorted features and outlines, traced with laudable feeling for the observance of the second commandment, (thou shalt not make any graven image) a chaotic assemblage of gaudy and crude colours, without harmony and without keeping. A very libel on the paintings of which they professed to be.'

Mrs Lowes in *Chats on Needlework* 1908 was even more scathing about them. For all Mrs Merrifield and others had said during the 1850s, pictures continued to be worked from similar designs for another fifty years. 'Think of the many years which English women have spent over wickedly hideous Berlin wool pictures, working their bad drawing and vilely crude colours into those awful canvases, and imagining that they are earning undying fame. During the middle and succeeding twenty years of the nineteenth century, the notable housewife of every class amused herself at the expense of her mind, by working cross-stitch pictures with crudely coloured wools which were supposed to represent the actual colours of Nature.'

Although this country abounded with superb examples of paintings, it was the romantic, sentimental, nineteenth century artist who caught the imagination of the Berlin pattern maker and the needle-

45 Small picture on single canvas, with painted brass frame; a photo-graph has been embellished with Berlin wool and silk embroidery, spangles and beads; probably German or Austrian

woman. The first patterns were made in Germany especially for the English market and at this time many German artists were producing the kind of picture which was popular, although the works of English artists were also in demand. Copies of excellent paintings were made, but they tended to be overshadowed by the quantities of poor quality work. The ladies who bought patterns of poor quality paintings had probably never seen the work of great artists, the critics abhorred copying of any sort of picture in needlework, but reproductions of pictures in one form or another were the only type of art the lower middle-class knew in their homes.

With all this criticism, it is only fair to say that many people genuinely admired the skill and industry of the ladies who worked these pictures. Although they were only copies, and not original work, the making of large complicated pictures with dozens of different shades was not a quick and easy task, as a large piece had about a quarter of a million stitches and with many pictures the standard of stitchery was excellent and the colours chosen with great care. Ladies often worked more than one canvas and there is on record one mammoth achievement from a lady living in a village in Middlesex. In this lady's house, room after room was filled with 305 cm × 244 cm (10 ft × 8 ft) canvases and every available drawer was crammed with examples of her work. After she had worked all the known subjects by Landseer and similar artists she had struck out on her own and copied pictures in *The Graphic* and *Illustrated London News Supplements*. There were scenes from the South African War such as *The Siege of Ladysmith* and *The Death of the Prince Imperial* with gruesome colouring on gigantic canvases. Her *pièce-de-résistance* was a copy in black, white and grey of the memorial statue of Queen Victoria.

Of the thousands of Berlin pictures that were produced only a few of the designs have survived in large numbers, although there are exceptions to this, for example St Fagan's Museum, Cardiff, has three copies of *The Shunamite's Son* and the whereabouts of four copies of the very large *Death of Black Douglas* are recorded. Dozens and in some cases hundreds of one design were probably made, but today it is some religious subjects which are most likely to be seen. It is difficult to know the reason behind the great popularity of these Bible pictures and it may be quite erroneous to believe that there were more copies made of them than other subjects in the last century.

The chromo-lithographed illustrations in the large family Bibles may have had something to do with the frequency with which the Berlin pictures were made, as many Bibles had elaborate copies of contemporary paintings or drawings on every page. The artists for these illustrations are rarely known but their style of work was very similar, with figures dressed in flowing robes and placed among palm trees whenever possible. Even when an indoor scene was portrayed a palm could be conveniently placed beyond a window or door, thus transporting the characters to Biblical lands; such as in the picture of *David and his Harp* and *The Raising of Jairus' Daughter*. It was so common to put palms in religious pictures, that it is fairly safe to guess an unknown scene is a Bible story if a palm appears.

Old Testament subjects have always been favoured by needle-women in preference to those about the Life of Christ, and this was so with Berlin pictures. Certain stories are met time and time again, especially representations of *Moses in the Bulrushes*. Some of the patterns suggest an Egyptian scene with a pyramid in the distance; others are set in a classical landscape and some look very English apart from an inevitable palm. A copy belonging to Mrs Eugene Levering of Baltimore, USA and illustrated in G. B. Harbeson's *American Needlework* has arum lilies, so beloved in the nineteenth century drawing room, growing from the Nile and the basket for Moses has a comfy, buttoned lining. Still, these pieces of artist's licence help to put such pictures firmly into the age when they were made. This particular picture measures 150 cm × 130 cm (59 in. × 51 in.) and was worked in 1865. It had been copied from a small picture which had been sent to console a mother over the loss of her small daughter, with the suggestion that to make a copy of it would keep her from brooding. It must be very well stitched for it won first prize when exhibited at the Maryland Institute of Art.

Many other stories from Genesis and Exodus were worked, especially scenes with Abraham, Isaac and Joseph. It is rare to find the people looking at all Jewish, but some artists did attempt to give the characters expressions—a picture of *Abraham offering his son on the Sacrificial Altar* in the Newark Museum, New Jersey, worked in 1843 shows a rather solid looking angel descending from the clouds and a look of real amazement on Abraham's face as he drops his knife.

Illustrations about David, Samuel and Daniel can usually be recognised. *Daniel in the Lion's Den* was very popular in America, as were all pictures of lions. They were worked at the time when men were bringing home trophies from Africa, although of course the pictures of wild beasts had no similarity with the tame creatures portrayed with Daniel. A decorative jug with a pattern in relief of *Daniel in the Lion's Den* was registered in 1859; it is very similar to the needlework pattern and may be contemporary with it.

Women were included in Bible pictures but usually in a mixed group. The only women to enjoy popularity in Berlin work were

46 Large picture *The Finding of Moses*; on single canvas in wool, silk, chenille and beads; grounding unworked; made near Maidstone, Kent, *c.* 1835 (page 18)

Ruth, Naomi, Rebecca, Rachel and the Virgin Mary. Nineteenth century Bible figures are usually dressed in a very uninteresting, conventional way, so unlike those in early needlework. For example, on an Elizabethan cushion at Hardwick Hall worked to represent the *Judgement of Solomon,* the ladies wear ruffs and farthingales and the men splendid doublet and hose.

When dating religious pictures, an unworked background probably denotes an early example, but the patterns were popular and available for many years, in spite of an answer to question in a magazine in 1861 which stated 'Scripture subjects are old fashioned and worked by our grandmothers, readers want something new'. Another correspondent to the same magazine who described herself as High Church asked for a pattern of 'Our Saviour on the Cross, with ground almost black, the body a beautiful flesh colour and blood streaming from wounds most natural'. The answer was that it was not right to publish such things in a magazine as 'these pictures are to be preserved in the inner most recesses of the home and are not to be trifled with or made common'. The picture to which the writer referred was probably a print published by Baxter in 1857 as *The Ninth Hour—* after a painting by Dürer.

Mrs Lowe had something to say about religious pictures 'Nothing was too sacred for the Berlin wool worker to lay hands upon. *The Crucifixion, The Nativity, The Flight into Egypt* and *The Holy Family* were not only supposed to show the skill of the worker, but also, the proper frame of mind the embroideress possessed. Pleasing little horrors such as *Head of the Saviour in His Agony* and the Virgin with all her tortured mother-love in her eyes were considered fit ornaments for the drawing room'.

Three religious pictures by great artists are frequently seen, they are *Sistine Madonna* after Raphael; *The Descent from the Cross* by Rubens and most often of all Leonardo do Vinci's *The Last Supper.* This last picture appears in all shapes and sizes but it is always recognisable, although the details vary considerably.

Another kind of wall decoration in Berlin work was a design of a religious text ornamented with a border of flowers or scroll work. *The Lord's Prayer, The Ten Commandments* and *The Creed* were made on enormous canvases, during the second half of the century.

The largest, most complicated and impressive pictures have historical places and events in England and Scotland as their subjects. Many of them were taken from well known paintings by nineteenth century artists and reflected the interest in history in all forms of the Arts. These subjects were popular in America for a time but they were gradually superseded by American landscapes by American

97

artists, especially scenes of the Civil War.

As with the original painting, size meant nothing, and it was usual to make the needlework the same size as the original picture. Many of these pictures were worked from very expensive patterns which were almost works of art in their own right. A special pattern could cost as much as £40 but the shop would buy it back when the work was complete and re-sell it at a reduced price. A needlework picture of *Mary, Queen of Scots* belonging to Mrs Zeigler, Long Island, USA, measured 182 cm × 152 cm (6 ft × 5 ft) and was started in New York in 1868. It took eleven years to complete, although during this time the lady made another smaller picture. She had a special room in her house devoted to the work so that the large array of wools, silks, chenille and beads was always to hand. With such a large picture, the worker had to keep the canvas rolled and work a portion at a time, otherwise she could not reach the centre.

The illustration of *Mary, Queen of Scots mourning over the Death*   47
of Black Douglas after the Battle of Langside is one copy of several excellent pictures worked from an identical pattern with slight variations of silk, beads and jewels. The artist was Regent Murray and the scene taken from Sir Walter Scott's novel *The Abbott*. The description in the book has been so faithfully reproduced in the painting and the Berlin wool picture, that it is possible to identify all eleven characters.

Several of Sir Walter Scott's novels inspired Berlin pictures, and although few have a title either in needlework or on the frame, it is possible to name them accurately. Scenes from *The Talisman, The Fair Maid of Perth* and *Rob Roy* were all made into Berlin patterns when the popularity of the novel was at its height.

Popular pictures were made of members of the Royal Family, from history and the present monarch. Mrs Brand at Glynde Place, Sussex, has a pair of Royal pictures. One is of Lady Jane Grey being offered the crown of England, taken from an oil painting by J. Mahoney (*d.* 1879), an engraving of this painting appeared in the *People's Magazine* 1867. With Lady Jane are her mother, husband, father and father-in-law. The stitchery is particularly fine and the details of the books on a table are represented in a most skilful way. The other picture is of Catherine of Aragon being told of her divorce and the stitchery on this is also exceptionally naturalistic, in particular the lace on the cotta of Cardinal Wolsey. The painter and the pattern maker were both great craftsmen.

The sad little picture of Charles I saying good-bye to his children   48
before his execution was surprisingly popular, and there were many pictures of Elizabeth I.

47 Very large picture *Mary, Queen of Scots mourning over Black Douglas
after the Battle of Langside;* worked by a fourteen year old girl in 1851;
wools, silks, pearls and jewels *Rochester Museum* (pages 19 and 98)

48   Small picture of *Charles I saying goodbye to his children*; a popular
picture *c.* 1840   *Mrs Violet Wood*

It was to be expected that portraits of Victoria and her family would be eagerly made. There were pictures of them together including copies of the famous Landseer painting, separate studies after the Baxter prints and probably the most popular of all pictures —pictures of the Prince of Wales as a child.

George Baxter published his first black and white illustration in 1827 and his first coloured print to imitate oil painting in 1829. He continued making them until his death in 1867 and many of his prints inspired Berlin pattern makers. Baxter obtained most of his ideas from other men's pictures and he was not a faithful copyist, often deviating from the original and sometimes, while retaining the main idea, entirely altering the design. It is not surprising that the Berlin patterns made from them were often very different from the original painting. His prints were small and cheap 6d to 2s od each for a picture 190 mm × 133 mm ($7\frac{1}{2}$ in. × $5\frac{1}{4}$ in.) in 1851—but clear and sharp, and they could easily be enlarged by the pattern makers. As well as portraits of the Royal Family, other Baxter prints which can be identified as Berlin pictures are views of Windsor, Osborne and Balmoral, Bolton, Netley and Tintern Abbey ruins; well-known beauty spots at Richmond Hill, Windsor Forest and Warwick Castle and pictures taken from the works of the Great Masters. Another Baxter print, which was made into a pattern, was a snow scene in the Alps; this subject was popular during the 1860s when the English, with the help of Swiss guides, developed the sport of mountain climbing.

As well as Baxter there were other men producing prints, some of which were doubtless suitable for Berlin patterns, especially the work of Le Blond, a French man living in England; Bradshaw and Blacklock; Dickes; Knoheim; Mansell and Vincent Brooks.

The work of Sir Edwin Landseer (1802–1873) has already been mentioned and many of his paintings were made into Berlin patterns, but it was with his studies of animals and birds that he achieved his greatest success with the Queen and her people. He was an extremely fine painter and in his choice of subjects he gave the people what they wanted. Among his paintings made into patterns were *The Monarch of the Glen, The Distinguished Fellows of the Royal Humane Society, Dignity and Impudence, There's Life in the Old Dog Yet* and portraits of the Queen's pets. His style was copied by lesser artists and the illustration of the deer made in Chatham, Kent, about 1890, belongs to such a copyist, and is now in Maidstone Museum, Kent.

Another artist who gave his animals similar appealing attitudes was Edward Lear (well known for his Nonsense Poems). His book of *Illustrations of the Family of Psittacidae or Parrots* (1830–32)

49 Small picture of Landseer's *Queen Victoria, the Prince of Wales and Princess Victoria c.* 1845 *Mrs Violet Wood* (page 101)

contained hand coloured lithographs drawn from life, and the superb colours were easily copied in brilliant Berlin wools. Such birds as the red and yellow macaw and the salmon crested cockatoo made attractive pictures for the wall or a pole screen. Parrots and other exotic birds had always been popular as pets in fashionable homes of the seventeenth and eighteenth centuries and had often appeared in needlework, but with the opening of the Zoological Gardens in

50 Large picture of Windsor Castle with a wreath of flowers *c.* 1860
Mrs Violet Wood

51　Large picture of *The Stag,* in the style of Landseer by a lesser artist; worked in Chatham, Kent, *c.* 1890　*Maidstone Museum*

Regents Park in 1828, many more people could admire their exotic plumage. John Gould, a taxidermist, decided to follow Lear's tracks and illustrated *Birds of Australia* (1837–8 and 1840–8) and *Monograph of the Ramphastidae of the Family of Toucans*; these were drawn from skins he had acquired, and many were made into Berlin patterns. Audubon's book on *Birds of America* was also used, his work can be distinguished from the other two artists because his birds are drawn surrounded by lush plant growth and sometimes in an elaborate landscape, whereas in the work of Lear and Gould the birds sit on a leafy branch only. The patterns made from the work of these three men are superior to many other similar examples.

Tropical birds, especially parrots, were very popular Berlin patterns, here and in America, right up to the end of the century. In G. B. Harbeson's *American Needlework* several parrots are illustrated in settings of tropical foliage or roses and arum lilies. A rather thin

52   Small picture of a King Charles spaniel on Java canvas; Berlin wool;
grounding unworked; originally had a scrolling border   (page 22)

parrot amid a few leaves from the Witte Museum, San Antonio,
Texas, has been worked on woollen cloth and the canvas threads
removed when the work was complete; another parrot on a cushion
belonging to a collector in Philadelphia has its wings raised for
flight, which is most unusual. It is very noticeable that the majority
of Berlin work in America was made in States bordering or close by
the Atlantic, suggesting the influence of Europe, even when American
patterns were produced.

In Berlin pictures of household pets, dogs outnumber all others
and many different breeds can be identified including St Bernard,
greyhound, King Charles spaniel, Skye, Cairn and sheepdogs. One
of the most popular dogs in Berlin wool was the King Charles spaniel,
probably due to *Dash* who belonged to Queen Victoria. He was often
portrayed on a tasselled cushion and there is a beautiful example on
flannel in the Victoria and Albert Museum. Although there were

53 Large picture on single canvas; *Girl with a Distaff c.* 1840
Mrs Violet Wood

54 Small picture of mallard ducks in cross stitch and raised wool work
with glass eyes; grounding unworked; on fine single canvas *c.* 1850
Mr C. F. Colt

designs of cats and cats and kittens appear in larger pictures, the
reason for their scarcity may be that they were still identified with
magic and thought by many people to be unlucky. The association of
ill-luck with many inanimate objects still applies today, although
cats appear to be widely accepted now.

The vast majority of Berlin pictures cannot be grouped in any way
but are just romantic or sentimental scenes both indoors and out,
which delighted the Victorian family and can be found as engravings

55 Small picture on single canvas; *Peasant woman and child c. 1870*

56 Picture on single canvas; made in Germany 1834 *Bayerisches* ▶
Nationalmuseum Munich, Germany

in many of the contemporary journals that were issued month by
month. There must have been thousands of patterns of different
pictures and new subjects are continually being re-discovered.

Most of the scenes were of English or Scottish life but there are European and occasionally Far Eastern landscapes. Albanian dancers were admired in Germany and several different pictures of them were made. *The Sicilian Maid* on the cheval screen, illustrated, is frequently seen and it is interesting to try and decide whether the slight variations in colours was due to the hand painting of the pattern or the choice of wools by the worker. Another foreign scene of which there are several copies, is of a most violent Eastern gentleman with a wooden arm riding a fierce charger. He is pointing at some ruins which are surrounded by oversized plants, and the whole composition is so badly drawn it is difficult to know why it had an appeal, unless it illustrated a forgotten popular story. A picture of Topsy and Eva chatting on a step from *Uncle Tom's Cabin* is recognisable because the story is still well known today.

57   Very large picture with vivid blue fountain and a border of flowers in raised wool work; *c.* 1860   *Mrs Humphrey Brand*

58   Small memorial in black and white with flowers in colour, 1886. It was not worked in a frame and bad shape was caused by working the top ▶ portion diagonally and the lower part horizontally   (page 78)

59   Picture on single canvas; made in France; wools and silk   *Mrs Humphrey Brand*

Scenes showing imaginary ballrooms with dancers in eighteenth century costume, idyllic Italian gardens, romantic musicians all had a place with the Berlin picture makers. They also worked scenes showing the lives of the very poor farm workers and fishermen, but in these pictures everything looks very cosy and nothing of the squalor that was actually existing was suggested. The cottager and his wife were surrounded with healthy children and contented pets, the fisherman was shown on a sunny day in safe harbour and even gypsies were made objects of envy with rosy children enjoying the freedom of the roads. One of the most attractive pictures of children is at Glynde Place, it is of two little girls playing with their pet rabbits while their setter dog is stretched out under a stool. An illustration of this design is in *American Needlework*.

There is a small group of pictures of ships worked by men using Berlin wools in long straight stitches, with the rigging worked afterwards in black thread. They are accurate representations of named sailing ships of the nineteenth century and by tradition worked by sailors actually on board them. Some people think this was not possible with the conditions below deck and believe that they were made by the sailors when on leave or retired. The picture of the ship 60 illustrated is in Rochester Museum, Kent, it is of HMS Racoon 1854, and the family to which it belonged were convinced it was made on board. Another magnificent picture in the same museum is of large spectacular sea battle, with several ships firing across the water. The gunfire has been suggested with red, orange and grey wool teased out into fluff and attached. The family of the man who made this picture were also quite definite that it was made aboard ship. Certainly, some may have been made in one place and some in another; it is difficult to prove anything conclusively.

60 Small picture of *HMS Racoon;* long stitches in Berlin wool with rigging in black thread; 1854; this picture was made on board the ship according to a descendant of the maker *Rochester Museum*

61 Small picture of Ireland in upright gobelin and long stitches; very
unusual design the sea is in shades of blue, the land in various brick red
colours, probably made before 1850 *Mr C. F. Colt* (page 54)

7   1851 Exhibition

Although there were exhibitions before 1851, both in England and in other European countries, they could not compare with the size and importance of 'The Great Exhibition of the Works of Industry of All Nations'. It was initiated by the Society of Arts under its president Prince Albert and held in the specially built Crystal Palace in Hyde Park. It was a resounding success, and was the forerunner of similar international exhibitions in Europe and America during the second half of the nineteenth century, and smaller shows, with local exhibitors, in towns up and down the country.

Some exhibitions were for commercial purposes only but others, including the 1851, had classes for amateur and professional work. Much can be learnt about the popular tastes of the people and the lavish designs of the few men who desired a new approach to art, by studying the elaborate and informative catalogues which were published at the time.

The catalogue of the 1851 exhibition contains much interesting information about Berlin wool work but unfortunately there are no illustrations. The section of the exhibition XIX concerning textiles is sub-divided:

A Tapestry (woven)
B Lace
C Tamboured work
D Embroidery
    (i)   Gold silver glass
    (ii) Silk for shawls, dresses, mantles, tablecovers
    (iii) Machine embroidery
E Fringes
F Industrial work
    (i)   Berlin wool work
    (ii) Needlework
    (iii) Miscellaneous

Most of the Berlin work was exhibited in the South Central Gallery, together with lace, tapestry and carpets. Work which had been produced commercially was not separated from entries by private individuals. In this gallery some of the large exhibits were hung from the girders as banners and the effect must have been most colourful and attractive.

It is not known whether all the entries which were offered were accepted, but there is no mention of a selection committee in the catalogue. There are several reasons for supposing that there was no standard for acceptance in section XIX. One, is the quality of the workmanship in a picture from Ospringe, near Faversham, Kent; which was at the Exhibition and is now in Maidstone Museum. This picture of a dog in plush or raised wool work, measures 305 mm × 254 mm (12 in. × 10 in.) and is worked on a fine single canvas. The dog is evenly worked, but the clipping of the wool shows no skill in shaping to give a three-dimensional effect. This was a difficult process and often done professionally when the work was finished. The 'sky' in the picture is a rather unpleasant brown and there is a black border in cross stitch with the stitches slanting in different directions. The border is such bad workmanship, that it might have been added by a different hand after the picture had been exhibited, but even discounting this, the remainder of the work is not of a high standard. Another reason is the large numbers of pictures with similar designs. The most popular was a representation of Leonardo da Vinci's *The Last Supper*. There were six entries with this title, but they may not have been identical; some copies were made with the length greater than the height as in the original painting and others were adapted to fit into a square. One, at least, at the Exhibition was not made in wool but worked in floss silk, it came from Twickenham; another from Market Harborough is described 'an impression of painting' and from Oxford came a copy with 500,000 stitches. There were four examples of *Mary, Queen of Scots mourning over the Dying Douglas at the Battle of Langside*; none were made in Scotland but by ladies living in London and Kent.

Several of the designs were probably taken from the popular prints published by George Baxter. Baxter exhibited at Hyde Park but his prints were not listed in the catalogue. Three Berlin pictures of the Royal Family from Staplehurst, Kent, and London were from a well known Baxter print, also a picture from Ireland entitled *Arctic Scene*.

All types of scriptural subjects were worked for the nursery or schoolroom and lower class families might have hung them in the parlour. Among those at the Exhibition were two copies of *Joseph presents his Father to Pharaoh*; this was a design which had been in favour for a long time. Copies can be found worked on silk with painted faces and the clothes worked in long stitches in wool or silk, dating from the first quarter of the century. From Wiltshire came *Esther and Mordecai* and an unknown lady sent 'three scriptural subjects worked from a pattern'. A picture from Bridport, Dorset is just called *A scriptural tapestry,* but was probably misnamed and is, in fact, Berlin work. A lady from Newcastle-upon-Tyne showed *The Arrival of Rebecca* after Schopins; *Bolton Abbey* by Landseer; Taylor's *Hawking Party* and Herring's *Feeding the Horses*. These were all complicated designs and probably large pictures.

Five Berlin wool carpets were exhibited and the one belonging to the Queen was described in detail. It was displayed hanging from the girders in the South Central Gallery and measured 914 cm long and 884 cm wide (30 ft long and 29 ft wide). It had been worked by 'The Lady Mayoress and 150 ladies of Great Britain'. Designed by an architect, John W. Papworth of Great Marlborough Street, it was made at the suggestion of W. B. Simpson of the Strand, who painted the pattern and supervised the making of the carpet. This great piece of work was undertaken to prove that the ladies of Great Britain were as competent at carpet making as the women on the Continent who made them on looms.

The design, part of which was also on show, had been painted as one picture and cut up into 150 squares, each of 610 mm (24 in.). These squares had the threads printed on them so that it was unnecessary to make a copy onto 'point' paper. The designs were geometric and floral connected by wreaths or bands of leaves and other foliage. The border contained the initials of all the 150 ladies incorporated in an heraldic pattern. It is an interesting fact that Papworth thought it necessary to publish a book on heraldry at this time, to help those people who had taken a renewed interest and acquired their own arms by diverse means—not always above board.

Unfortunately, the Queen's carpet has been lost or destroyed and there is no pictorial record of the great achievement, but it certainly emphasised what was written as an introduction to this section in the catalogue. 'Works are displayed which have occupied the unwearied leisure hours of some years and they display a large amount of industrial perseverance'. The *Art Journal* of 1851 reported the Queen's carpet contained 17,340,000 stitches when completed.

Of the four other carpets listed, much less is known. One is described as 'A contribution carpet, worked in Dublin for the benefit of The Irish Society for promoting the Scriptural Education of the Native Irish'. It was made by 115 ladies in 91 squares and took six months to make. The designs on the squares were each of a different plant, bird or landscape. Another carpet was of 30 squares and had been worked by one lady who lived at Minster on the Isle of Sheppey, Kent. Both these carpets have also disappeared without a trace.

Two Berlin wool carpets were exhibited by German manufacturers, but nothing is known about them.

Among the exhibits were several which were not described as Berlin work, but nevertheless were probably worked on canvas from Berlin patterns. One example was 'Flags of All Nations, designed in London and worked with wool, silk, chenille and beads'. The whereabouts of this particular picture is not known, but the design remained popular throughout Victoria's reign and was still being worked in the 1900s. There were variations in detail, but the flags were usually arranged in a semi-circle, with or without a border of leaves.

A piece of work described as 'embroidery' usually implied Berlin work and an example was exhibited by Brooks of Kennington. It represented English History with the Royal Arms in the centre and the initials crown and badges of Victoria, Albert and the Prince of Wales. Around were worked various symbols connected with the Royal Family: a harp for Ireland; pomegranates for Catherine of Aragon; the trunk of a tree for Edward III; a portcullis and fleur-de-lis for the Tudors; a rose on a sun for the Plantagenets; an empty pea shell for Richard II; crossed feathers for Henry VI; a dragon for Cadwallader and Wales and a white horse for Saxony and the House of Brunswick. No mention was made of the size of the embroidery, but from such a detailed description it suggests a large piece.

Several patterns for making flowers from Berlin wool can be found in woman's magazines of this time, and some were made up and on show. There was an exhibit from a lady in Taunton, Somerset, which had been knitted and another from a manufacturer in Hatton Garden, London, that showed Berlin wool flowers in various containers—cane baskets; porcelain vases; a rustic vase and several metal holders. They were all enhanced by the use of green woollen turf, which was made by knitting a strip in the appropriate colour which was then dampened, pressed and unravelled and the crinkly wool obtained was sewn or glued around the flowers.

Manufacturers displayed designs, canvasses and completed work. Hill and Company from Worcester and Great Malvern, employed two sisters to make their designs which included pieces suitable for furniture—ottomans, screens and chairs, also pictures of Windsor Castle from Baxter's print, Tintern Abbey ruins, Witley Court and a miniature portrait of Leonardo da Vinci. Another manufacturer from London informs us that Mrs Marsh of Stoke Newington worked the six Berlin pictures displayed on his stand.

Some exhibitors claimed to show only original work. Tarin of Camden Town was designated 'designer and inventor of Berlin wool needlework' and Rodolphe Heilbronner (German) of Regent Street, London, showed designs on a new kind of canvas.

It is known that not all Berlin pictures were made from printed patterns. Some of the earliest ones may have been drawn in ink onto the canvas from paintings in the manner of eighteenth century designs; a few were painted in full colour onto the canvas by talented ladies who designed their own work. Very very few printed patterns for pictures exist today and they are conspicuous by their absence in museum collections. One probable explanation of these missing designs is that they were in a ragged state by the end of their use; another is that once a large picture had been worked the needlewoman would not want to work the same pattern again, whereas the floral and geometric patterns were kept in case they could be used for something else, in much the same way knitting patterns are kept today. Another reason for their rarity is given in the description of the work of Andrew Hall of Manchester who 'invented' the idea of printing the design for a picture onto the actual canvas, and in so doing made a paper pattern unnecessary. It is not known how popular this process became in the nineteenth centuty, for although it is much used today for canvas work designs, most Berlin wool pictures that have worn patches do not show any design on the canvas.

A 'new' invention of 1851 by Bondy of Rotherhithe, London, was an idea to help ladies who found difficulty choosing the correct shade of wool to match the colour in the paper pattern. A glance at many needlework pictures will make it obvious that it was indeed a difficulty, especially with flesh tones and some really ghastly examples were worked. (In a copy of Queen Elizabeth and Raleigh at a quayside, the colours are so crude, it is difficult to believe the worker ever thought them to be correct.) The process, evolved to overcome this difficulty, was to print the Berlin pattern in black and white with each square having a letter for the colour and a number for the shade. On a separate sheet of paper all the colours and shades were listed in rotation with a small piece of wool the exact colour glued by the code. No doubt, this was an expensive way of achieving a good colour combination, but a mistake was almost impossible.

The majority of Berlin work on show from Great Britain was from England but there were a few pieces from Ireland, Scotland and the Channel Isles.

Of the foreign countries exhibiting it is not surprising that Germany was well represented.

Five pattern makers from Berlin are listed. A. Todt does not give the subjects of his designs but examples of his work in the Victoria and Albert Museum are floral sprays and borders painted in bright colours. They are all fairly small designs and a colour code is given at the bottom of the design—this is a strip containing one square of each of the colours to be used. Gruenthal showed *Lady Jane Grey*; *Washington*; *David and Saul*; *Madonna and Child*; *A Boy at Play* and 'a pair of shaped panels for the back and seat of a chair'. The only pattern by Gruenthal in the Victoria and Albert Museum is printed on stiff card with a geometric design in crude colours. Neie and

Seiffert and Company had unnamed paper patterns. Louis Gluer exhibited *The Descent from the Cross* after Rubens; *George Washington* and *Albert, Prince of Wales.* Rudloff Brothers, *Cardinal Ximenes; Laban and Jacob* and *Hagar in the Desert.*

Konig of Berlin had on show a carpet in cross stitch, a bed screen and a fire screen in *petit point* on silk canvas. Schleuss showed embroideries in imitation of mosaic, but it is not known what these looked like.

Two amateur needlewomen from Berlin sent pictures, one sent a Scottish landscape and a scriptural subject *Moses in Minia*; the other had made an attractive picture in plush stitch (raised wool work) cut into a realistic three dimenstional effect.

From Lubeck (NW of Berlin) Carl Stolle sent various cotton and silk canvases with designs and perforated cardboard for a bottlestand, watch case, visiting card case, calendar and a basket. A very interesting piece of embroidery from this firm was described as having been commenced and supplied with wools, silks and pearls for its completion. Spiegal and Company, designer and manufacturer also sent similar 'commenced embroidery'. The Museum Fur Kunst and Gewerbe, Hamburg, not far from Lubeck, have no record or examples of this type of work but the Bayerisches National museum, Munich, supplied the following information about *'angefangene Stickereien'* which literally translated means 'begun or unfinished embroidery'.

'Report on the Grand Duchy of Baden Crafts Exhibition Karlsruhe 1847 . . . the so called *angefangene Stickereien* was given by the city of Munich (a firm of Kley and Son, Mannheim was mentioned) . . . with special respect for his efforts in delivering the piece of *angefangene Stickereien* which is a thing of absolute beauty and for making this article in the Grand Duchy, and which up to now has only belonged to Berlin!'

A manufacturer of canvas had various embroideries on show from Hesse (SE of Berlin) and from Saxony (the original home of Berlin wool); a mention is made of local zephyr wools in different sizes being dyed in Berlin by Bergmann and Company.

A mill near Vienna, sent Berlin wool and worsted yarns to the Exhibition.

The only other European country exhibiting was Belgium, with some scriptural pictures and pictures in Gothic style from Louvain, and several different items from Brussels including Berlin wools, a worked cushion, a picture and a pair of needleworked braces.

From America came a lone entry *The Raising of Jairus' Daughter* worked in Boston, Massachusetts.

8   Stitches and other uses of Berlin wool

Two names which frequently occur when referring to any type of canvas work are *petit point* and *gros point*; both are mis-used terms.

Petit point is a simple sloping stitch over one vertical and one horizontal thread on single canvas or pair of threads on double canvas. It may slope upwards from right to left but it usually goes from left to right. It can be a very small or a large stitch depending on the mesh size of the canvas. It is also known as *tent stitch* and in America as *needlepoint*. It is very suitable for details and fine work but whole pieces for furniture may be worked with it. Berlin pictures are often worked in this stitch.

Gros point is a cross stitch worked over one or two vertical and two horizontal threads. It is easiest to work on double canvas when each cross covers one pair of vertical and one pair of horizontal threads. The size of the stitch varies with the mesh of the canvas as in *petit point*. It is a hard-wearing stitch and was frequently used with Berlin wools. For a period of time after 1856, all canvas work in cross stitch was called Berlin work in America; this was the date when the wools were first imported from Germany.

To summarize these two stitches which were used for the majority of all Berlin wool work; *petit point* is not necessarily a small stitch and *gros point* simply means cross stitch. Although many kinds of stitches are possible on canvas and they were attempted on nineteenth century samplers, very little variation was seen on Victorian work. The large and elaborate pictures and the carefully shaded floral designs were only capable of being worked in cross or tent stitch but many simpler patterns would have been entranced by the use of other stitches and have been more interesting to work. Magazines and books realized this and tried to encourage the use of new stitches by giving them wonderful, descriptive names, but to very little effect.

It is difficult to give the correct name for a particular stitch because of the practice in magazines of giving a different name to an already known stitch to suggest that it was something new. Some of the stitches that they published had no name at all and were just engravings of the finished result with instructions for working. The names of Berlin stitches were just as obscure in American books, with such names as *Czar stitch, Princess Frederick stitch* and *Victoria stitch!*

The instructions given in Mrs Henry Owen's *The Illuminated Book of Needlework* in 1847, list thirty-three canvas stitches. At the beginning she writes that she is not going to commit the errors of previous books and her stitches will not be difficult to work correctly. However, they are very muddled and to make matters worse, the drawings do not match the numbers in the text. With directions such as these, it is hardly surprising that the ladies preferred to do their work in tent stitch.

The following is the list of stitches from this book. Mrs Owen's instructions and where possible, her illustrations are given. (See diagrams iii, iv, v.) The modern name for the stitch, if there is one, and remarks are in brackets.

1	Tent	Use a frame and work grounding on the cross
2	Cross	
3	Straight Cross	The stitches are vertical and horizontal
4	Windsor	See diagram iv, page 124
5	Pavilion	See diagram iv. Gold beads can be added
6	Josephine	Known as Hungarian or Mosaic
7	Berlin	Use contrasting colours (a Florentine scallop)
8	Czar or Economic	See diagram. Use gold thread between each row
9	Irish	Upright Gobelin or Brick stitch
10	Willow or Basket	See diagram. Colours do not matter
11	Long plait	Striking effect if gold or silver thread is used between rows
12	Feather	The centre is stitched with gold, silver or silk thread (vertical knitting stitch)
13	A la Vandyck	See diagram. Very beautiful with careful choice of colours and gold or steel beads
14	Point	Use shades of the same colour for bags (Florentine)
15	Square Plait	See diagram. Bright colours should be placed in opposition
16	Gobelin	
17	Perspective	See diagram. Fill the centre with silk
18	Star	A bead in the centre of each star worked in various silks
19	Velvet	Work with a line of Czar stitch in between and cut loops with a pen knife (Plush stitch)
20	Serpentine or Spiral	(There is no diagram and the instructions are not explicit)
21	Double Star	See diagram. Use bright colours with a centre of silver, gold or steel beads
22	Crossed Long	(There is no diagram and the instructions are not explicit)

23 Fancy	See diagram. Fill centre with coloured silks
24 Lace stitch	Work with black Chantilly silk, a resemblance to pearl edge can be given by taking two threads straight, beyond the pattern. See description in Chapter 4, Samplers
25 Princess	See diagram. Use alternate colours
26 Hohenlinden	See diagram. Named after the German princess whose beauty captivated the bravest and most accomplished men of the day. (Instructions not clear, it may be (i) or (ii))

CROSS STITCH

HALF CROSS STITCH

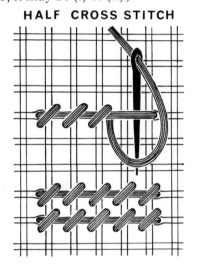

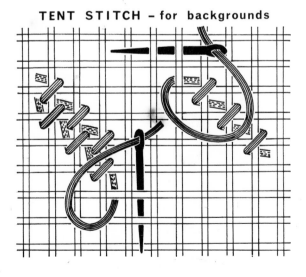

TENT STITCH – for backgrounds

– for details

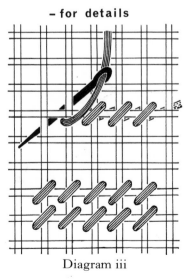

Diagram iii

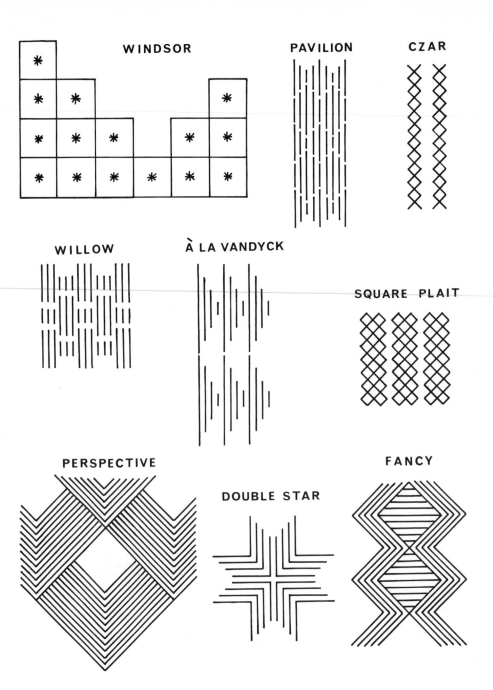

WINDSOR PAVILION CZAR

WILLOW À LA VANDYCK

SQUARE PLAIT

PERSPECTIVE FANCY

DOUBLE STAR

Diagram iv

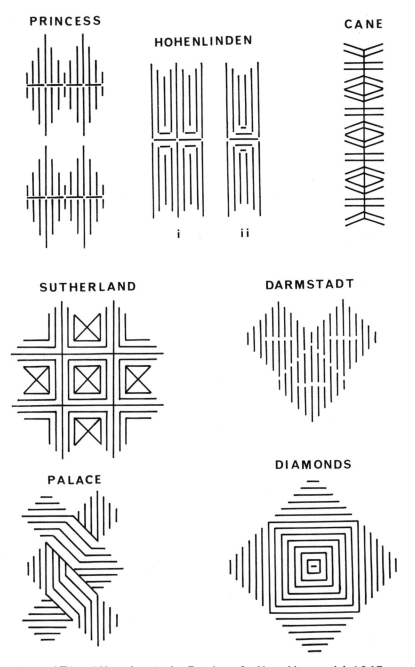

PRINCESS

HOHENLINDEN

i   ii

CANE

SUTHERLAND

DARMSTADT

PALACE

DIAMONDS

from 'The Illuminated Book of Needlework' 1847

Diagram v

27	Cane pattern	See diagram. One row cane pattern, four rows Irish stitch in shaded colours very quick and effective
28	Sutherland	See diagram. Beads in the spaces, can be worked in gold or silver threads
29	Darmstadt	See diagram. Work the space in the centre with beads
30	Palace pattern	See diagram. Never wearies the eye, possessing within itself a great variety of outline and so natural in its arrangement that notwithstanding the angularity of its character, it never offends by obtrusiveness of one portion to another
31	Plaid	Tartans should be worked in cross stitch
32	Diamond	See diagram. Finish round the edges of diamonds with steel, silver or gold beads
33		A strange diagram of a pattern without name or instructions.

Although most of these stitches were not in general use, several can be identified on samplers, and the lace and florentine stitches were used on larger pieces of work. There was such a wonderful range of shades possible in Berlin wool that examples of florentine patterns are most attractive on chairs and stools.

Raised wool work or plush stitch

The use of this stitch in Berlin wool produced a realistic three dimensional effect with a soft fluffy appearance. It must not be confused with raised work which is another name for seventeenth century stump work. The idea behind the Victorian work probably came from the French tapestry weavers who evolved a method of making a velvet-like pile in the eighteenth century but something very similar had been used long before on stump work embroidery to create a realistic effect. There is little doubt that raised wool work was a copy of this as the method for achieving the effect was so similar. Raised wool work was introduced during the 1840s and was worked more frequently than might be supposed for such a complicated stitch.

Although this book does not attempt to show how to do all types of Berlin work, the method of sewing raised wool work is included, as many people are mystified by it and do not understand how it is produced. Directions for working the stitch are to be found in lady's magazines and occasionally books. Various methods are suggested but all of them recommend the use of a gauge or mesh. Originally netting meshes were used which were flat pieces of wood about six inches long and of different widths, but later improved gauges were made especially for the work. Some were made of steel sharpened at one end and sold for 1s 6d in 1863, but in *The Illuminated Book of Needlework* by Mrs Henry Owen another kind was mentioned which cut the wool without cutting the fingers. This had a deep groove at one end into which a blade could be fixed when the gauge was ready to be withdrawn.

The method for making a mat decorated with raised wool work roses was given in *The Englishwoman's Domestic Magazine* January 1863. 'Thread as many long needlefuls of wool as there are shades. Hold the mesh in the left hand, lay it on the canvas and with the right hand hold the needle and put it through the canvas from underneath. Put the wool round the mesh, work a single stitch and then cross it. One loop must then be thus formed for each stitch. The shade of wool must be changed as indicated in the pattern, but the wool must not be broken off each time but carried along the wrong side of the work. The work is done in straight rows and when one row is finished the mesh is drawn out, the sharp knife at the end cutting the loop.'

In America it is sometimes called clipped work but usually plush stitch. A method of working in *American Needlework* by G. B. Harbeson has been taken from a needlework book of 1858.

'Plush stitch
One or more prominent objects in the design are raised. The plain parts in cross stitch should be worked first. Thread needles with various shades of wool and obtain flat netting meshes. Begin at the left hand corner, lowest part, with the proper shade, the wool being double. Bring the needle up between the two upright threads of the first cross stitch, take the needle to the left, bringing the needle out in the same hole. Put the wool round the mesh and take a stitch to the right. The needle coming out again in the same cross. Thread round the mesh, and take a stitch from the hole of the last, down to the right, the wool to the right of it. Thread round, one to the right cross, the wool to the right of it. A figure V is thus formed on the wrong side. When done, gum the back and cut the loops.'

It is possible to work a raised stitch with close herringbone. The rows are worked one upon the other, each successive row being wider than the last until a thick band is produced. This is cut down the centre and the tufts are longest at the outside, forming a rounded shape. Another raised effect can be produced with velvet stitch. Close herringbone and velvet stitch are described in a modern book, Mary Thomas's *Dictionary of Embroidery Stiches*, Hodder and Stoughton.

Embroidery paste or gum was occasionally put onto the back of ordinary Berlin wool embroidery but it was essential with raised wool work to anchor the cut threads. However an advertisement from a Berlin wool Repository in Edinburgh in 1845 suggested paste was not necessary if a special method of doing the stitch was followed but unfortunately the recommended method was not shown.

The paste was either put straight onto the back of the work or onto a piece of tissue paper which was stuck onto the wool. A nineteenth century recipe for making a paste used 1 oz size 1 oz sugar candy and a small piece of alum. These were covered with cold water and after four hours, 1 oz flour was added and then the mixture was boiled. Another recipe used flour and size and after boiling a teaspoon of essence of cloves was added for a preservative.

The final process in raised wool work was to sheer the wool to produce contours and to give the bird or flower a natural appearance. This was skilled work and badly executed examples were just flat and fluffy like a patch of cotton wool; the very worst ones even made the design unrecognisable. Because of the difficulty of clipping correctly, magazines suggested it was advisable to take the work to a shop which specialized in needlework and have it done by an expert.

Raised wool work was more suitable when used on some subjects than on others. Among the most successful were some varieties of flowers and birds. Roses and cacti were well suited to the three dimensional effect but when used on arum lilies they lost their waxy appearance and were not improved. Parrots were favourite designs for all types of needlework and many were beautifully stitched in raised wool work, the illustration of the parrot and cactus flowers is extremely fine work and the cutting of the wool has been expertly accomplished. Most birds were worked full size and as well as tropical varieties, hawks, pheasants and ducks sit realistically amid foliage, peering out with glass eyes.

Another use of the stitch was to imitate fur, both on animals and as fur trimming on costume. When ermine was imitated the result was most convincing and was often used to embellish the large historical and religious pictures together with beads, pearls and metal threads.

Special patterns for the work were not needed and any suitable design could be used. The few which were published specifically for it, just stated in words that it was for raised wool work and sometimes they included a small drawing of the finished article showing the special effect of the raised portions.

It is very difficult to date examples but very few were made before 1845.

Large picture of a parrot with cactus and other flowers; in cross stitch and
raised wool work with many beads; on fine single canvas *c.* 1850; grounding
unworked; originally a cheval screen   (page 91)

Plate 3

Wool work flowers

A mid-Victorian idea introduced a new technique with Berlin wool, it was the creation of realistic arrangements of woollen flowers under glass shades. It was already popular to have delicate or valuable ornaments and natural history specimens under these, and the rounded glass domes have preserved many interesting pieces of Victoriana from dirt and breakage. The shades could be really small affairs, no more than 152 mm or 203 mm (6 or 8 in.) across and 254 mm (10 in.) tall, to quite outrageous objects as high as 914 mm (36 in.). The flowers were usually arranged in a basket and were occasionally grouped with wax fruit, small birds' eggs or sea shells. The inside of the basket or the ground on which it stood was sometimes decorated with green wool to represent grass (see chapter on 1851 Exhibition). The edge of the glass was covered with a fluffy braid or plush to act as a dust excluder and the woollen flowers were protected from everything except the sunlight.

Favourite flowers were roses, lilies, pansies and orchids, but instructions were published for many other kinds including camellias, daisies, convolvulus, poppies, hyacinths, geraniums and lily of the valley. Although the flowers were worked in their natural colours, the groups were predominately white, red and mauve.

If a brightly coloured arrangement is seen, it has a certain charm and one must admire the skill and patience necessary to create them.

There were various methods for making the flowers but most of them were made on a specially shaped piece of wood with a foundation of wire, and the wood was removed when the flower was complete. In Caulfield and Saward *Dictionary of Needlework* there are instructions for making a pansy, convolvulus, daisy and rose.

'A convolvulos
Take a round shaped piece of wood and in every scallop lay a line of fine wire bringing all the ends to the back through the centre hole where they can be twisted together. Thread a needle with white wool, fasten in the hole in the wood and pass it round in circles between wire and wood. As each wire is reached, make a stitch over it so as to enclose it, then carry on. As the work progresses, each time round is slightly larger until half the rosette is covered. Then continue with pale blue wool up to the top. Cut wires at the back and turn in the ends to secure them, the flower will assume a trumpet shape when released. Make stamens by covering wire with yellow wool. Wind green wool round the ends of the wire to make stalk.'

62   The illustration of the basket of wool flowers includes roses, convolvulus, lilies, pansies, hyacinths, a bee-orchid, fuchsias and

62 Basket of wool work flowers under a shade *c.* 1860   (page 129)

foliage all worked in such a naturalistic manner as to be immediately recognisable.

Knitting, crochet and netting with Berlin wool

It was suggested that knitting gave manual occupation which occupied the mind enough to beguile it without cares or producing fatigue. When a lady was too indisposed to embroider with her Berlin wool work, either through advancing years or illness, knitting could be employed. It was not suggested that knitting was only suitable for such people, as it was done by all ladies, but it was not so demanding as a difficult Berlin pattern.

Berlin wool was not strong but its soft texture made it suitable for knitting bonnets, ruffs, scarves, doilies and even a boa. Knitting patterns in the last century were a very far cry from those published today and some of them had very muddled directions.

Crochet could be worked with Berlin wool and alternatively, crochet patterns could be used for canvas work designs. Some of the designs for crochet on squared paper are difficult to distinguish from a black and white Berlin pattern. Bags of all descriptions, cushions, table covers and slippers were among ideas suggested for crochetting with thick Berlin wool.

Berlin wool could be used to make runners, mats and scarves by netting.

Fringes were made by knitting or crochetting in Berlin wool and it could be used to make the fluffy tassels or balls for the edging. Instructions for making these in single wool are found in several books, together with a suggestion to make the balls look like daisies and use them to decorate the edges of mats.

Costume and accessories

A few articles of dress were made with Berlin wool work and men received most of these as gifts from the ladies. Most middle class bachelors, about 1850, possessed something made by an admiring relation or friend.

Magazines were full of suggestions, but the wool slipper seems to have been the most popular choice from the number which remain today. The shape of 'carpet' slippers is somewhat unfamiliar before they are made up, and a pair of these are illustrated. When the needlework was complete, it was taken to a shoemaker to be lined and soled. The charge was about ten shillings at the end of the nineteenth century and would be about £25 today if a shoemaker could be persuaded to do the job. Slippers were made in all sizes and the Bath

Museum of Costume have an attractive collection of them. There is one pair of men's slippers with a fine design of a water birds and another pair are completely worked with beads. Among the children's slippers on show, which are mostly floral, is one pair with what looks like a pixie on each front. Although there were many different patterns published, the most attractive had small repeating designs. However flowers and animals were popular, especially a fox's mask, even though Mrs Merrifield in the *Art Journal* of 1851 writes 'It is just bad taste to adorn the front of a slipper with a fox's head and see it peeping from under the master's trouser and about to advance on the visitor'. The strange use of a slipper pattern is sometimes seen when it has been used on a cushion or a child's sampler. Although Berlin work was as popular in America as England there was always a time lag between the introduction of new ideas and patterns. A slipper with a fleur-de-lis design appeared in the *Englishwoman's Domestic Magazine* in 1862 and was published in *Peterson's Magazine* (USA) 1867.

63   Pair of carpet slippers not made up; in wool and silk on black ground *c.* 1880

64   Some handsome waistcoats were made from Berlin patterns on canvas for the two fronts. Most of the designs were small repeating patterns and tartans. Some appear to have been made by working a large piece of canvas which was then cut out and made up by a tailor.

64   Waistcoat with fronts in Berlin work; unused *Maidstone Museum*

It is difficult to date wasitcoats but many of them were made during the first half of the century. The tartan patterns were probably the result of the Queen's interest in Scotland and they were usually accurate, although some can be found in unusual colours. Waistcoats worked in diagonal stripes gave an interesting effect when they were reversed on each front.

Smoking caps were part of every man's attire indoors and although most of those which have survived are not in Berlin work, instructions for making them on canvas and adorning the top with a tassel were published. Directions for making one in 'Turkish stitch' were given in 1864. This stitch was supposed to have originated due to the popularity of Dadood Pasha, a well liked literary man who joined the Turkish Cabinet and was attached to the Ottoman Legation in Berlin. It was said that he was only the second Christian to join the Council of the Ottoman Empire. The stitch was introduced into England through pieces of work sent from Berlin for ladies to copy.

These 'useful knick-knacks' made for men were embroidered with designs which appealed to the lady who made them and no thought was given to masculine taste or to the possible embarrassment caused to a bachelor if he owned a cigar case embroidered with a dove and blossoms and 'Don't forget me' added in cross stitch.

Bags of all shapes and sizes were made; the largest of them was the 'railway or carpet' bag and was used by men and women. It was a 65 useful and capacious article lined with striped ticking and bound with leather. It had leather handles and often straps and buckles, which were attached by the local saddler, but the bag illustrated was sewn together by an amateur. Designs for the wool work vary but stripes were very popular.

Watch stands were made for the drawing room and bedroom in many materials; those made in Berlin work are known as watch pockets or watch hooks. Watch pockets could be hung on or beside the bed or downstairs and the watch could be popped into the bag when not required, the watch hook was an improvement on this as the pocket watch could be hung on a brass hook which was sewn onto the front of a flat piece of needlework, stiffened with cardboard. A favourite method of embroidering both of them was with a design of beads threaded in strings and sewn down over a padded shape, with the background worked with wools. The watch pocket illustrated is 66 very large and was used well into this century.

65   Carpet bag in wool bound with leather *c.* 1870   *Maidstone Museum*

136 66 Watch pocket in red wool and beads *c.* 1860 (page 134)

Berlin work for the church

Hassocks, banners and carpets were made for the church by energetic parishioners but most of them have long since disappeared. Designs for hassocks published by Weldon's about 1880 were predominately geometrical, but religious symbols and flowers were used at this time as well. Designs were usually in cross stitch but one pattern for a hassock suggested using feather, long and short stitch and french knots. The design has a cross in light brown with a crown of thorns in yellow on a background of dark brown. No size is given but from the engraving it appears to be worked on single canvas. A very few hassocks made of Berlin wool can still be found in churches but the uninteresting choice of colours coupled with dirt and fading have made them most unattractive now.

An advertisement in the *Art Journal* of 1847 states that designs suitable for the church were available from England, France and Germany, for altar hangings and carpets with the design drawn on the canvas. They could be purchased already started and this probably meant a quarter of the design was complete so that copying was easy, or the whole design was worked and the lady who bought it only had to fill in the background and then proudly give it to her church.

Church banners made in Berlin work were very heavy to carry, but they were made, often with very poor designs. They needed a stiff interlining to prevent them curling at the edges, but the additional weight made this impracticable and surviving examples do not hang well. The designs were adapted from religious pictures or drawn by an amateur artist, the favourite subjects being Christ on the Cross and Christ's Head adorned with Thorns. It is possible to distinguish a church banner from a pole screen as most of those worked for the church had lettering on them.

9 New work and restoration

New work

Many women, and men as well, find the repetitive stitches used on an elaborate piece of canvas work very relaxing. It is not easy to reproduce Berlin patterns from original Berlin charts as they are extremely difficult to find, but there are many alternative ways of creating attractive needlework.

The most important requirement is to be able to recognise good design whether it is an old one or a modern pattern. If an authentic reproduction nineteenth century design is to be chosen it is essential to look at examples in museums, books and antique shops to become familiar with the style before deciding on a particular pattern.

For the ambitious person who wants to create an original Berlin pattern in nineteenth century style, ideas may be found on such things as crochet patterns, cross stitch charts, samplers and, best of all, on Tunbridge Ware. Many of these designs are indistinguishable from Berlin patterns and with Tunbridge Ware they were often taken from actual charts, so that with patience, the borders, floral bouquets and even elaborate scenes can be recreated in colour. Designs are best worked out on graph paper ten squares to the inch and coloured with paints or crayons, but for those who insist they cannot draw anything, it is possible to work out a motif for a repeating pattern with needle and thread on a sample piece of canvas and experiment with size and colour.

Printed coloured charts are still manufactured in limited quantities but suitable ones may be difficult to find.

The embroiderer who does not want the bother of following a chart or counting can choose between using a painted canvas or one which has the design indicated by long threads of the appropriate colour and known as a *tramé* or *trammed design*. Both types are sold as 'tapestries' and are usually on double thread canvas with the wools pre-selected, if required. Although there are plenty of good designs, poorly drawn and crudely coloured ones are offered for sale, so it is worthwhile seeking a specialist needlework shop with a large stock from which to choose.

The choice of design is very wide indeed and all the types available in the nineteenth century are still being produced today with a very large selection of floral patterns.

The choice of colours to use is difficult and will depend on several things. Do you want the work to look like a new piece of Berlin needlework with clear, brilliant colours or an old piece with the appearance of age in more subtle shades? Is the most important reason to find colours to blend with existing furnishings or do you want to recover an antique chair as a focal point? There is a very wide range of colours in embroidery wools and it is possible to find most of the shades which were made in Berlin wool although certain ones may be difficult such as vermilion, dark jade green and pinky-purple. Some shops stock imported wools which come in different colours to English wool and sometimes knitting wool or stranded cotton can be used. Whatever thread is chosen it is important that the stitch completely covers the canvas, otherwise the result will be patchy and weak. Do not let the choice of colours be dull; a careful choice of background colour can overcome this. Always buy sufficient wool to complete the work as the shades sometimes vary with different batches.

Choose a strong canvas as it is the basis of good work but avoid a harsh one which is unpleasant to handle. An elaborate design needs a canvas with even threads and easily defined holes. Much of the prepared canvas is on a ten holes to the inch mesh which is very suitable for cross stitch or half cross stitch in tapestry wool. Very dainty designs can be worked completely with stranded cotton on a finer canvas, about sixteen holes to the inch. Double canvas is easier than single for cross stitches as the holes are more clearly seen. Tent stitch is equally satisfactory on either type.

Suitable beads to use on an elaborate design are not easy to find as the number of shades available in each colour are not sufficient to produce good effects.

Canvas work is more even if worked in a frame but if a worker finds this awkward, very good results can be obtained when it is held in the hand. When worked in a square frame (never use a round one, except for very small pieces of work which do not reach the edge of the frame) the canvas must be stretched so tightly that the needle cannot go in and out with one movement. It is necessary to use both hands, the right one to push the needle down from the top and the left to push it up from underneath. Some workers find a thimble on both hands helps them.

The method used by the best workers in the nineteenth century was to start at the top of the design and work downwards so that none of the wool became rubbed or dirty. However most workers prefer to start at the centre and work outwards. If working from a chart, tack the centre horizontal and vertical lines onto the canvas before commencing the pattern.

Use a needle without a point. They are tapestry needles and can be bought in a variety of sizes; 18 to 22 are suitable for most woollen threads. The wool should be able to move freely in the eye of the

139

needle, but it should not be larger than necessary. Only use a short length of thread, not more than twelve inches and move it occasionally in the needle while sewing so that it does not wear thin, or this will show on the finished work.

With cross stitch and horizontal rows of tent stitch always sew in the same direction, beginning each new row at the same end. If rows are worked backwards and forwards they will appear uneven.

Cross stitch should be worked by completing each stitch before passing on to the next. Do not work half the stitches all along the row and then come back and cross them (diagram iii).

If tent stitch is used for the background, as much of it as is practicable should be worked diagonally (diagram iii).

Begin each new length of thread with a knot on the right side of the work about one inch from the first stitch. As the work progresses, this thread will be covered and the knot can be cut off when it is reached. To finish off, run the thread under several stitches on the back, but do not go over and over as they would make a lump.

All work is improved by stretching; it takes the place of ironing which makes canvas work look flat and lifeless. Stretching is essential for work that has been held in the hand to restore it to its original shape. Use a wooden board or make a rigid rectangle with four pieces of wood. Put a piece of old white cloth on this and lay the canvas face down. Fasten one straight edge with small nails about 25 to 50 mm (1 to 2 in.) apart. Pull the canvas into shape and nail across the diagonal. Continue nailing all round, making sure it is the correct shape; some alteration in the positions of the nails may be necessary. Do not worry if it is puckered. Thoroughly damp the whole canvas and leave it to dry. Remove all the nails and it should look smooth and in its original shape, but if it is still not quite right, repeat the process.

Restoration of Woolwork

If the work is very dirty it is well worthwhile to wash or dry clean it at home.

First test for colour fastness by damping a piece of white material and pressing it firmly onto the back of the wool. If there is no discolouration, other than dirt, prepare a large bowl or sink of cool water to which a little salt and liquid detergent have been added (washing up liquid is ideal). Put the woolwork on a piece of sheeting to support its weight throughout the washing, rinsing and drying. Dip up and down gently but do not attempt to squeeze or rub. Rinse in cool water the same way. Dry as quickly as possible away from direct heat or sunlight. A great deal of moisture can be extracted by putting the work between two towels and pressing gently, and afterwards putting it onto a layer of newspaper which is changed as it absorbs the moisture. On no account should any piece of old needlework be pegged on a line.

Do not iron, but if the wool work is out of shape, stretch it on a board or frame. (See *New work*, p. 140.) It may be possible to nail the work onto a rough wooden frame before washing and remove it when it is dry and this will prevent any shrinkage or puckering which is important if the needlework came from a piece of furniture.

If the colour runs, it must not be washed. Remove as much loose dirt as possible with a very soft baby's hairbrush or by shaking carefully, then lay on a flat surface and cover with magnesium carbonate, a white powder obtainable from a chemist. Leave for several hours and then shake off. This should have absorbed much of the grease and dirt and can do no harm to the most delicate fabric.

After the work has been cleaned, examine the canvas on the back and if it shows any signs of weakness completely cover the back with *Copydex* which will secure the wool in position. If the canvas is very weak and especially if there are any bare patches which will need re-sewing, immediately place the wool work onto a piece of new, closely woven material which is slightly larger than the old work and it will adhere to the *Copydex*. New canvas is not the best material to use for backing.

It is not necessary to put the wool work in a frame to mend it, although if the worker is used to embroidering on one, it will probably speed the work.

The choice of a suitable thread to mend bare patches is most difficult, correct colour is all important and sometimes a knitting wool may be better than an embroidery one. Remember some of the highlights may have been sewn with beads or silk originally. Use blunt ended tapestry needles.

Always have the stitches slanting in the same direction. It is usually advisable to use the original type of stitch for the repair, but with cross stitch it is worth experimenting first. If the new wool is slightly too thick, the stitch will appear lumpy if worked correctly and the use of a half cross stitch may be preferable (diagram v).

While restoring wool work, never fold the canvas. Always keep it flat or wind it round a cardboard tube or roll of newspaper.

A slightly different method of restoration is used if the design is on a canvas which did not have the background stitched. Washing would remove the stiffening from the canvas and therefore dry cleaning is advisable. Do not fix a new backing with *Copydex*. A piece of carefully selected material should be placed at the back and only attached with stitches at the edges where necessary to keep it flat. By choosing a very light backing the work will appear brighter but any ends of wool and long stitches on the underside will be more noticeable. Try out several shades of very pale greys and creams and choose the one which will lighten the wool work without showing up the threads on the back.

Pictures

It is unwise to remove old needlework from its stretcher—the wooden frame to which it is nailed.

It is not usually necessary to do any cleaning to pictures, other than to remove dust, but if the picture has been glazed, the glass may be very dirty on the inside. All old needlework pictures should be glazed to preserve them.

Small holes in the wool work will need some attention and an exact colour match with new threads is needed. However a method of improving the appearance of the work which may be less obtrusive than a conventional repair for the occasional missing stitch, is to mix up the exact shade with water colour paint and touch up the canvas.

When the picture is re-fixed in the frame, seal the back with a sheet of brown paper glued into position.

Beadwork

Restoring beadwork can be very tedious work but well worth the time spent on it as almost perfect results can be obtained.

Beads do not fade but some will crack with age and fall off, while metal ones can rust and disintegrate the thread and the canvas. Large bare patches are caused by the thread rotting.

Where beadwork has part of the design in wool, it must be treated as wool work, but all bead designs can be given different treatment if they are very dirty. Choose a warm, sunny day and spread a piece of old sheeting on the ground. Lay the beadwork on this and gently scrub with cool water and detergent using a soft brush. Rinse by pouring plenty of water over it. Dry as quickly as possible as for wool work, but it can go in the sun. If the design has rusty beads, extra care is needed to prevent them staining the work and it may be advisable to remove them before washing.

After it is dry, remove any loose beads. As the beads are so heavy and the old canvas must be weak, always cover the back with Copydex and then attach it to a piece of new, strong, closely woven material.

It is very important not to fold beadwork.

The best beads for replacement are old ones. Sometimes a very old and worn piece can be cut up to re-use the beads and occasionally boxes of old beads can be found. New beads in a limited range of colours can be bought from some embroidery shops.

The best thread for sewing beads onto old work is old, fine linen thread, if it is still strong, as it will be dark with age. If a white linen thread is used it is a good idea to stain it with tea or coffee and dry it without rinsing. Sewing cotton is not as good as linen thread but will do if nothing else is available. *Sylko* is not strong enough and pure silk is only suitable for small, light-weight beads. If the thread is waxed it will be stronger.

Beading needles size 10 or 12 will pass through the holes of most Victorian beads.

A word can be added about restoring bead trays which are often used as wall decoration. It is difficult to take them apart to replace missing beads by sewing and small bare patches can have beads glued into position with *Seccotine*.

Appendix A

Berlin patterns given during 1861–4 by the *Englishwoman's Domestic Magazine*. The words in brackets are the author's comments. The patterns were printed in full colour.

1861

Feb   Border for a bracket, window cornice or table cover. Floral design with a fancy-shaped edge to be worked in bright colours and finished with tassels. Grounding can be in beads.

April   Small floral pattern suitable for a cigar case, pocket book, spectacle case etc. To be worked in floss silks on fine canvas.

May   Bouquet of flowers suitable for a banner, with a suggestion for re-arranging the design to fit a sofa pillow. Silk canvas and wools can be supplied for 9s 6d or cotton threads for 6s.

July (a) Bouquet of flowers for an urn or teapot stand. Grounding can be of beads. A suggestion for repeating the design for a larger article.

(b) Directions for making a netted antimacassar darned with wool from a Berlin pattern. (There is an interesting letter printed from 'Contessa' who writes that she made a pair of oriental slippers from a previously published pattern. 'The officer (oh! happy son of Mars) who has become their fortunate possessor is obliged to keep them under lock and key, lest they should be feloniously abstracted by his envious comrades.')

Aug   A bead mat for a flower vase to catch dampness or stray leaves. White, crystal and steel beads are used with a scarlet wool centre.

Nov   A medallion pattern suitable for chairs or if repeated could be used to border curtains. The design of roses is outlined in filoselle silk on a grounding of blue, green, scarlet or white. (There is a note to the effect that medallions are more fashionable than a running scroll.)

1862

Jan   Bouquet of roses for a chair seat. The number of skeins of wool are given. For the violet flowers purchase ingrain Berlin wool which does not fade or fly as is generally the case with this colour.

Feb   An opera hood made in alpine rose and partridge Berlin wool. The fluffy appearance is produced by working over a frame and then cutting as in a daisy mat.

Plate 4   Beadwork design for a table top *c.* 1845   *Victoria and Albert Museum*

March   Watch hook with raised leaves of white, gold and steel woollen grounding. To transfer the pattern lay canvas over the illustration and mark with pen and ink. The leaves are padded with wadding which is covered with a piece of stiff writing paper.

May   A wreath of flowers in white, gold and steel beads for a music stool. The design for this and the watch hook in March have been done by the first German and French artists, who have spent months working it out—no trouble or expense has been spared.

June   Bouquet of roses—companion with the one in the January issue. Pattern by W. Dickes, 5 Old Fish Street, London (very good quality). Groundings can be maize blue, black or white.

July   Geometric pattern with roses for a sofa pillow, footstool etc. One quarter of the design given. (This is a French pattern of poor design and printing by Dupuy Passage du D'esir 3 Paris.)

Aug   Oriental design for music stool (ghastly colours and poor design.)

Nov   Slipper with Prince of Wales' feathers design in blue with white, steel, crystal and black beads. Printed by Duplay, La Maderie, Paris. (An answer to a correspondent suggests the following suitable gifts to make for a gentleman—braces, smoking cap, slippers, tobacco pouches, cigar cases.)

Dec   Bouquet of flowers for a chair or stool.

1863

Jan   Round mat with raised wool work. This is now very fashionable, especially roses. The trimming of the work is difficult and many ladies send work to be professionally finished. (Full instructions follow).

Feb   Watch pocket design of leaves and flowers backed with paper and covered with beads threaded in long strings.

March   Toilet cushion in beads and wool.

April   Slippers with a floral design.

May   Bouquet of flowers to match companion pattern published December 1862.

June   Watch hook in raised wool work.

Aug   'What-not' in wool and beads for hanging on the wall to hold papers, cards or sewing implements. If the wall paper is neat use solferino or crimson grounding, if it is gay a quiet grounding should be selected.

| Oct | Antimacassar, netted in white or black and darned with black, magenta or orange wool. |
| Dec | Slippers with raised wool work and beads. It is suggested the work is clipped flat not shaped (design not known). |

1864

| Jan | Banner with a small repeating fleur-de-lis design worked with white, grey and black beads on a grounding of cross stitch with a bead fringe. (This is a very simple pattern.) |
| Feb | Cushion in wool and steel buttons. The invention, of Hutton and Company, London, is novel, effective and easy to accomplish. The buttons are made with a double prong and are put into the work when complete, the prongs bend back and are secured. 4d a dozen. |

1864

March	Drawing room mat with a floral pattern in wool on a grounding of crystal beads. It is to be mounted in a gilt frame with the work stretched over a piece of wood and screwed in.
April	Border for curtains or table cover in Levithan work (this was a large stitch worked on a coarse canvas).
May (a)	Sofa pillow in a floral design (this pattern had been hand painted).
(b)	Footstool an unusual elliptical design which costs 7s 6d plus 3s 8d for the embroidery materials.
June	Railway Travelling Bag with a design of an engine in beads on a wool ground.

On canvas No 42 the bag will be 15 in.

26 the bag will be 22½ in.

45 (in levithan stitch) 27 in.

| Aug | Slipper with English and Danish flags, oak leaves and acorns. (Pattern painted by hand to commemorate the marriage of the Prince of Wales—later King Edward VII to Princess Alexandra of Denmark in 1863.) |

Appendix B

Berlin patterns given during 1871–4 by *The Young Englishwoman's Magazine*. The words in brackets are the author's comments. The patterns were coloured in various ways or given in black and white.

1871

Jan   A square design for a cushion (no illustration available in the magazine, it was given with the separate supplement containing fashions, fancywork and music).

Feb   An anemone in Berlin wool to be worked on a round flat wooden mesh with holes all round and in the middle. Fasten on crosswise a thick thread, fasten yellow wool in centre and turn it in coils round centre, passing between mesh and thread. Obtain a flat circle 3 in. to 4 in. across, pass some split wool 4 or 5 times across the coils to keep them together. Draw up one tighter to form scallops, cut away the thread, fasten it to the mould. Draw out one petal and fasten on to wire. (Much clearer directions for making these flowers can be found in other books.)

March   A sofa cushion design with an all-over small design. Materials obtainable from Mesdames Le Boutillier, 125 Oxford Street, London.

April   Three vandyke borders for brackets with a twisted bead fringe. Can be made completely in beads.

Aug   Three small repeating designs suitable for any use.

Sept   Tiny wreath of flowers for a pincushion with crocheted monogram in the centre.

1872

Jan   A very small border.

April   A cushion in raised wool work called plush stitch (the leaves have fluffy middles with a good diagram of how to do the stitch).

May (a)   Pattern for a breakfast tray with a geometrical design in wool and beads.

    (b)   Description and diagram of how to do long cross stitch and double cross stitches.

1872

June   Pattern for a tea cosy with a design of arum lilies and roses. (The design is coloured all over with powder paint or pastels which rub off when touched. The blue background is particularly unstable and messy.)

July	Designs on single canvas using long stitches.
Aug	Six different stitches including shell, milanese, oriental, cashmere. (Although seen on samplers it is very rare to see them worked on whole pieces. None of the stitches are actually named.)
Oct	(a) Gentleman's boot in a striped design.
	(b) Star repeat pattern for a sofa cushion.
Nov	Pattern for a Prince of Wales Ottoman by Mme Figuier, Paris. (A hand coloured plate in violet, blue, magenta, green and black.)

1873

Jan	Coloured geometric design for a tray in beads and wool made in Strasburg.
Feb	Black and white design for a cigar case, blotting book cover or flower stand.
March	Drawing room chair seat with arum lilies and roses hand coloured for wool and beads.
May	Pattern for Louis XII chair to fit sides and top with flowers coloured with the same messy substance as the tea cosy, June 1872.
June	Border (printed with very violent colours) suitable for table cover, curtains or chair back (a low chair).
July	Border designs in black and white.
Aug	Royal Stuart tartan—a coloured German pattern to be worked in double cross stitch. (*Good Wives* was published as a serial, beginning with this number.)

1874

Jan	A very small pattern for petit point.
Feb	Coloured repeating pattern for a Louis XIII fender stool. Medallions of fleur-de-lis and griffons on red and green with black background.
May	Chair seat '*The May Fair Mode*' (a very unsuitable and crowded design).
July	Watch pocket in beads and red wool.
Sept	The Khiva Lambrequin (a badly coloured and most unattractive design).
NOTE	The following year the *Young Ladies Journal* had even fewer needlework patterns and more stories.

Appendix C

Advertisement of Wilks Warehouse in the *Art Journal* January 1851. British Gobelin Patterns for canvas work.

'This well-known series of patterns (so called from being designed and published by the British Gobelin Warehouse, 186 Regent Street) is constantly being enlarged. These patterns were originally issued with a view to their exclusive application to crochet but, having been brought into such general use for canvas work, all earlier designs have been recomposed to suit them equally to both purposes. They were the first and are still the only succesful application of crochet to the effective representation of flowers, birds and ornamental design. Bold in effect and easier to work from than the Berlin patterns, they form the most elegant article of drawing room furniture introduced for many years. On canvas the most brilliant effects are produced by working the centre pattern in any one colour, say gold colour, and grounding it in some other colour darker, say crimson or green or blue, and working the border in a much lighter shade of the same colour as the ground, varying the chromatic or to harmonize with the furniture of the apartment, arrangement to the taste of the worker. An inspection of the *Worked Specimens* exhibiting at the warehouse in Regent Street, will show that a new style of needlework has at length been introduced which from its beauty, simplicity, great facility of execution, economy and universal applicability must eventually supersede most others.

The subjects are flowers in bunches or in vases and baskets, birds, butterflies, etc. for the centres with rich borders to each.

There are several sizes, *viz :*

1 Small square for cushions etc, 6d each or free for 8 stamps.
2 Small oblong for chair backs etc, 1s each or free for 14 stamps.
3 Large oblong for ditto, horizontal for sofa backs etc, 2s each or free for 30 stamps.
4 Large squares for table covers, ottomans etc, 2s 6d each or free for 36 stamps.

Three sheets of Doyleys, four on a sheet, several sheets or semées and running patterns and sheets of borders for general purposes, and for the enlargements of the small squares, 6d the sheet or free for 8 stamps.

The principal subjects are:

1 Small squares—lily, passion flower, camelia, carnation, geranium, hearts ease (pansy), wild rose, datura (thorn apple) convolvulus, ivy, moss rose, woodbine, gloxinia, honeysuckle, basket of flowers.

2   Small oblongs—lily, passion flower, wild rose, cyclamen, poppy, convolvulus, vase with tulips, vase with carnation, each surrounded with an elegant border.

3   Large oblongs

	Centre	Border
No 119	Vase of flowers	Etruscan
120	Carnations	Ivy leaves
141	Vase of flowers and butterfly	Etruscan
142	Parrot on branch	Wild roses
143	Roses grouped	Wild roses
144	Basket of flowers horizontal	Etruscan
145	Group of flowers horizontal	Ivy leaves

4   Large squares

No 151	Group of flowers	Vine leaves and grapes
152	Bird on branch	Vine leaves and grapes
153	Lyre with laurel wreath	Wild roses
154	Cockatoo on branch	Wild roses

Also two *prie dieu* chairs, backs, seats and cushions to match. They represent Gothic Tracery—the one set filled with passion flower, the other set with the lily. Each chair, with its cushion consists of 3 large plates.

Any one of the six patterns 2s or free for 2s 6d, two free for 4s 6d, three for 6s 6d, four for 8s 6d, five for 10s 6d, six for 12s 6d. Postage all free beyond the first.

Every design is original, executed on the premises and to be had at no other house.'

Appendix D

The Husband's Complaint

I hate the name of German wool, in all its colours bright;
Of chairs and stools in fancy work, I hate the very sight;
The shawls and slippers that I've seen, the ottomans and bags
Sooner than wear a stitch on me, I'd walk the streets in rags.

I've heard of wives too musical,—too talkative—too quiet,
Of scolding and of gaming wives and those too fond of riot;
But yet of all the errors know, which to the women fall;
For ever doing fancy work, I think exceeds them all.

The other day when I went home no dinner was for me,
I asked my wife the reason; she answered, 'One, two, three,'
I told her I was hungry and stamped upon the floor
She never even looked at me, but murmured 'One green more.'

Of course she made me angry,—but she didn't care for that,
And chatters while I talk to her 'A white and then a black
Seven greens and then a purple,—just hold your tongue my dear,
You really do annoy me so, I've made a wrong stitch here.'

And as for conversation with the eternal frame,
I speak to her of fifty things—she answers just the same!
'Tis 'Yes my love, five reds and then a black, I quite agree with you,
I've done this wrong, seven, eight, nine, ten, an orange then a blue.'

If any lady comes to tea, her bag is first surveyed,
And if the pattern pleases her, a copy there is made.
She stares too at the gentleman, and when I ask her why,
'Tis 'Oh my love, the pattern of his waistcoat struck my eye.'

And if to walk I am inclined ('Tis seldom I go out)
At every worsted shop she sees Oh how she stares about
And there 'tis 'Oh! I must go in that pattern is so rare,
That group of flowers is just the thing I wanted for my chair.'

Besides the things she makes are such touch-me-not affairs,
I dare not even use a screen,—a stool,—and as for chairs!
'Twas only yesterday I put my youngest boy on one
And until then I never knew my wife had such a tongue.

Alas! For my dear little ones, they dare not move or speak:
'Tis, 'Tom be quiet, put down that bag, Harriet, where's your feet?
Maria standing on that stool—it was not made for use,
Be silent all—three green one red and then a puce.

Ah! The misery of a working wife, with fancy work run wild,
And hands that never do aught else for husband or for child;
Our clothes are rent and minus strings, my house is in disorder,
And all because my lady wife has taken to embroider.

I'll put my children out to school, I'll go across the seas
My wife's so full of fancy work, I'm sure she wont miss me;
E'en while I write she still keeps on her one, two three and four,
'Tis past all bearing, on my word, I'll not endure it more.

The Wife's Answer

Well to be sure, I never did, why what a fuss you make,
I'll first explain myself, my dear, a little for your sake:
You seem to think this worsted work, is all the ladies do,
A very great mistake of yours, so I'll enlighten you.

I need not count, for luckily, I'm filling up just now,
So listen, dear, and drive away those wrinkles from your brow—
When you are in your study, love, as still as any mouse,
You cannot think the lots of things I do about the house.

This morning after breakfast I heard the children spell,
And I'm teaching little Mary to gather and to fell;
I've paid my washing bill, and then I went to see
What contents in the larder for our dinner there might be.

I've finished Tommy's pinafore, and fed the green canary,
I've hemmed a duster, and I've made a bonnet cap for Mary.
I've practised that concerto thing, you thought so very fine.
I've written all the notes, as well to ask our friends to dine.

I've filled my vases with fresh flowers, so fine they are and full,
And after that—I will confess—I sorted out my wool;
I've read that paper setting forth the sweet confiding trust,
Husbands should cherish for their wives, and think it very just.

I've settled all my weekly bills, and balanced my accounts,
With a little lot of German wool to make up the amounts,
Ah! now at last my reasoning convinces you I know,
That pleasant smile—and yes, my love—it does become you so;

Besides, to tell the truth, all the worsted work I do,
My bags, my cushions and my chairs are in compliment to you.
I made a set of night-shirts, and did you not declare
That the rending of the calicoe was more than you could bear.

I knit some lamb's wool stockings, and you kicked up such a rout,
And asked how soon my ladyship was going to have the gout!
So now, my dear, entirely to please you I declare,
I've worked this splendid arabesque upon my vesper chair.

Two hearth-rugs and an ottoman, seven chairs and after that,
I hope to do some groups of flowers, and a handsome carriage mat;
Enough of banter; yet believe one word before we part—
The rest perhaps was fable; but this is from the heart,—
The loving wife, right cheerfully, obeys her husband still,
And will ever lay aside her frame to meet his lordly will.

From '*A History of Needlemaking*' by M. T. Morrall 1852

Bibliography

Mansions, Men and Tunbridge Ware, Younghusband, Windsor Press 1949

Victorian Embroidery, Barbara Morris, Herbert Jenkins 1962

Dictionary of Needlework, Caulfield and Saward, London 1882

Chats on Old Lace and Needlework, Mrs Lowe, T. Fisher Unwin 1908

National Museum of Wales Catalogue of Samplers and Embroideries

Samplers, Averil Colby, Batsford, London, Branford, Mass., 1964

The Perfect Lady, C. Willet Cunningham, Max Parrish 1948

The Antique Dealer and Collector's Guide, July 1966

The Art of Needlework, Countess of Wilton, London 1840

Victoriana, Violet Wood, G. Bell and Son 1960

Illuminated Ladies Book of Useful and Ornamental Needlework, Mrs Henry Owen, 1847

Art Needlework, Mrs Townend, Collins 1910

Aunt Fanny's Album, Powell Perry, Perry Colourprint

Weldon's Practical Needlwork

Needlecraft Artistic and Practical, Butterick Publishing Co., New York 1889

Lady's Handbook, Florence Hartley, Philadelphia 1859

Victorian Furniture, F. G. Roe, Phoenix House 1952

Official Descriptive Catalogue of the Great Exhibition, 1851

English Furniture, E. T. Joy, Batsford 1962

The Victorians, Sir Charles Petrie, Eyre & Spottiswoode 1960

Edward Lear's Parrots, B. Reade, Duckworth 1949

Bead Embroidery, Joan Edwards, Batsford, London, Taplinger, New York, 1966

Needlework as Art, Lady M. Alford, London 1886

George Baxter, C. Courtnay Lewis

Contemporary periodicals

The Englishwoman's Domestic Magazine

The Young Ladies Journal

The Ladies Treasury

EveryWoman's Encyclopaedia

The Girl's Own and Woman's Magazine

The Queen

The Young Englishwoman's Magazine

The Girl's Own Annual

Sylvia's Home Journal

◀ 67   Berlin wool work on flannel; the canvas threads were removed when the embroidery was complete   *The National Museum of Wales, Welsh Folk Museum*

Suppliers in Great Britain

The following supply a variety of canvases, frames and many shades of wool. Prepared canvases are available and customers' own designs can be produced from pictures, and sketches. Most firms will stretch and mount finished work.

Mrs Mary Allen
Turnditch, Derbyshire

Art Needlework Industries Ltd
7 St Michael's Mansions, Ship Street, Oxford

B. Francis
4 Glentworth Street, London NW1

Harrods Limited
Brompton Road, London SW1

Christine Riley
21–3 West Port, Arbroath, Angus, Scotland

Ladies Work Society
Delabere House, New Road, Moreton-in-the-Marsh, Gloucestershire
and London showroom at
138 Brompton Road, London SW3

John Lewis
Oxford Street, London W1

Mace and Nairn
89 Crane Street, Salisbury, Wiltshire

The Needlewoman Shop
146 Regent Street, London W1

Nottingham Handicraft Company
Melton Road, West Bridgford, Nottingham

Royal School of Needlework
25 Princes Gate, London SW7

Mrs Joan Trickett
110 Marsden Road, Burnley, Lancashire

Betty Veal
Waterloo Buildings, London Road, Southampton, Hampshire

Suppliers in the USA

American Thread Corporation
90 Park Avenue, New York, NY

Hollander Bead and Novelty Corporation
25 West 37 Street, New York 18

Bucky King Embroideries Unlimited
121 South Drive, Pittsburgh, Pennsylvania 15238

The Needle's Point Studio
1626 Macon Street, McLean, Virginia 22101

Tinsel Trading Company
7 West 36 Street, New York 18, NY

Yarn Depot
Sutter Street, San Francisco 94102

Crewel and tapestry wool

Appleton Brothers of London
West Main Road, Little Compton, Rhode Island 02857

68 Pole screen worked in wool with a grounding in white wool; fine double canvas *Mrs Humphrey Brand* (page 22)

Index

Ackerman, importer, 8
Alford, Lady M., *Needlework as Art* 1886, 17
American Needlework 1860, G. B. Harbeson, 24, 95, 104, 113
Art Journal
  1849, 30, 50, 63
  1853, 74, 192
Art of Needlework, The, Countess of Wilton, 7, 8, 76
Art Needlework, Mrs Townend, 34
Arts and Crafts Movement, 62

Baldwin, J. & J., 15
Banner screens, 78, 79; *35, 37*
Baronial Hall, series, J. K. Knight & Co. 1840, 28
Baxter, George, publisher, 101
Beads, 18–20
Beadwork design, *plate 4*
Beadwork, restoration of, 142
Bedford, J. & C., 76
Bell pulls, *41*
Berlin wool, derivation, 7
Berlin wool, 13
  colours, 15
Berlin Wool Repositories, 13, 14, 18, 30, 76
Borders, 32; *18, 19*
Brand, Mrs Humphrey, 19, 21, 22, 75, 76, 90, 101; *32, 38, 56, 57*
Buttericks, *Needlecraft Artistic and Practical* 1889, 23

Cardboard work, 23
Carpet bag, 134; *65*
Carpets, 86–87; *42*
Canvas, 20–22
  in America, 23

Caulfield & Saward, *Dictionary of Needlework,* 13, 26, 74, 129
Chairs, 64–70
  early Victorian, *24*
  mid-Victorian, *24; 25*
  prie dieu, 16, 63, 64, 67; *26*
Chaise longue, 61, 68, 70
Chats on Needlework 1908, Mrs Lowe, 92
Chenille, 18
Cheval screens, 32, 68, 77, 109; *31, 34, plate 3*
Church work, 137
Cole, Miss Edna M., *11–14, 35*
Collenson, James, *The Empty Purse,* 50
Colt, C. F., 77; *37, 54, 61*
Costume and accessories, 131–136
Cushions, 21; *38*

Designs, hand-coloured, 7, 8, 17, 27
  printed, 8, 27
  beadwork, *plate 4*
Dictionary of Needlework, Caulfield & Saward, 13, 26, 74, 129
DMC cotton threads, 17
Dyes, 15, 16
  aniline, 15, 16

Empty Purse, The 1857, James Collenson, 50
Englishwoman's Domestic Magazine 1862, 14, 28, 32, 72, 87, 132, 144–146; *15, 16*
Everywoman's Encyclopaedia 1911, 15
Exeter, Marquess of, 20

Falbe, G. E., 32; *plate 2*
Fender stool, *30*

Footstools, 72; *29*
Frames, 24–26; *1*
Furniture, 61–67
  Regency, 61, 67
  Victorian, 62

Girl's Own Annual, 32
Glüer, Louis, *8*
Glynde Place, Sussex, 19, 21, 22, 75, 76, 90, 112
Graphic, The 1883, 72, 94
Great Exhibition, 62, 86, 115
Grubb, F. C., of Banbury, 26

Hamlyn-Williams, Lady Mary, 70
Hand (face) screens, 79; *33*
Hand Book of Needlework 1843, Miss Lambert, 7, 8
Hardwick Hall, 97
Harbeson, G. B., *American Needlework* 1860, 24, 95, 104, 113
Hartley, Florence, *Lady's Handbook,* 20
Hertz & Wenener, pattern makers, 22, 30, 32; *6, 17, plate 2*

Illustrated Girl's Own Treasury, 62
Illustrated London News Supplement, 94
Illustrations of the Family of Parrots, Edward Lear, 101

Kent, Mr D., *3, 4, 5, 6, 7, 17, 18, 19*
Kershaw, Leese & Sidebottom, 27
Klickman, Flora, *Little Girl's Sewing Book,* 15
Knight, J. K. & Co., *Baronial Halls* series, 28

Lambert, Miss, *Handbook of Needlework* 1843, 7, 8
Ladies Hand Book 1859, 18
Ladies Treasury 1867, 16, 32, 87
Lady's Handbook, Florence Hartley, 20
Landseer, 90, 94, 101; *49* style of, *51*
Lear, Edward, 101
Linwood, Miss, 88
Little Girls' Sewing Book, Flora Klickman, 15
Lowes, Mrs, *Chats on Needlework* 1908, 92

Magasin des Demoiselles 1851, 30
Merrifield, Mrs, criticism, 92
Morris, Barbara, *Victorian Embroidery*, 25, 27
Morris, William, 17, 62
Mount Vernon Ladies Association, 25; *1*
Museum of Costume, Bath, 13, 79, 86, 132
Museum of Wales, National Welsh Folk Museum, *22, 25, 26, 27, 31, 41, 67*
Museum, Belfast, 25
    Brecon, 59
    British, 27
    Maidstone, 60, 96, 101; *33, 51, 64, 65*
    Newark, 95
    Rochester, 113; *36, 47, 60*
    St Fagan's, Cardiff, 16, 20, 47, 50, 52, 53, 54, 59
    Tunbridge Wells, 74
    Ulster, 92
    Wells, 79
    Witte, Texas, 105
    Victoria and Albert, 20, 22, 24, 30, 39, 59, 60, 67, 70, 76, 78, 86, 89, 105

Needlecraft Artistic and Practical 1889, Buttericks, 23
Needles, 26
Needles Excellency, The, 27
Needlework as Art 1886, Lady Alford, 17
Needlework for Student Teachers 1894, Amy Smith, 14
New work, 138, 139

Owen, Mrs Henry, *Illuminated Ladies Book*, 7

Pattern makers, 32
Patterns, hand-coloured, 7, 8; *1, 2, 3, 4*
    printed, 8, 17, 27–46; *11, 13, 15*
Patterns, Philipson's, 7, 8
    chair, *8*
    for beads, 20
    slippers, 132; *10, 63*
    Wittich, publishers of, 8
Paton and Baldwins, 14
Paton, John, 15
People's Magazine 1867, 98
Perkin, Sir William, 16
Peterson's Magazine, USA 1867, 132
Pictures, 11, 17, 88–114
    behind glass, 16
Potter, C. H. & E., printers, 28
Pole screens, 33; *36, 68*
    Regency, 61, 62
Purcell and Dolan, Mesdammes, 30

Religious subjects for pictures, 11, 88, 89, 90, 95, 97; *43, 44, 46*
Registration of Designs Act, 27
Royal School of Needlework, 17
Restoration, 140, 143

St Alban's, Duchess of, 13
Samplers, 47–60; *20, 21, 22, 23*
Screens, 75–83
Settees, 70; *27, 28*
Slippers, patterns, 132; *10, 63*
Smith, Amy, *Needlework for Student Teachers*, 14
Stitches, 121–127

Tarn & Company, Schools suppliers, 14
Threads, 17, 18
Todt, A. & G. E. Falbe, pattern makers, 32
Townend, Mrs, *Art Needlework*, 34
Tunbridge Ware, 10, 72, 74

Waistcoat, 13, 133; *64*
Washing work, recipe, 17
Watch pockets, 134; *66*
Weldon's Practical Beadwork, 19
Wilks, Mr T., of Regent Street, 8, 30
Warehouse, 149–150
Wilcockson, Mrs, supplier, 14, 87
Wilton, Countess of, *The Art of Needlework* 1840, 7, 8, 76
Wicht, Carl F. W., pattern maker, 32; *plate 2*
Wittich, L. W., 8, 28, 30, 32, 67; *4, 5*
Wood, Henry, *A Useful Modern Work . . .*, 63
Wood, Mrs Violet, *28, 29, 30, 34, 42, 44, 48, 49, 50, 53*
Woolwork flowers, 129; *62*

Young Englishwoman's Magazine, 32, 147–148
Young Ladies Journal 1872, 26, 32, 76, 90; *10, 11, 13*